Naomi Pfitzner · Kate Fitz-Gibbon ·
Sandra Walklate · Silke Meyer · Marie Segrave

Violence Against Women During Coronavirus

When Staying Home Isn't Safe

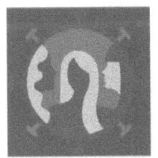

palgrave
macmillan

Naomi Pfitzner
School of Social Sciences
Monash University
Clayton, VIC, Australia

Kate Fitz-Gibbon
School of Social Sciences
Monash University
Clayton, VIC, Australia

Sandra Walklate
Department of Sociology, Social Policy
and Criminology
University of Liverpool
Liverpool, UK

Silke Meyer
School of Health Sciences - Social
Work
Griffith University
Brisbane, QLD, Australia

Marie Segrave
School of Social Sciences
Monash University
Clayton, VIC, Australia

ISBN 978-3-031-29355-9   ISBN 978-3-031-29356-6   (eBook)
https://doi.org/10.1007/978-3-031-29356-6

Cover illustration: Pattern © Melisa Hasan

This Palgrave Macmillan imprint is published by the registered company Springer Nature Switzerland AG
The registered company address is: Gewerbestrasse 11, 6330 Cham, Switzerland

CONTENTS

CHAPTER 1

Contextualising COVID-19: Domestic and Family Violence During Times of Crisis

Abstract This first chapter sets the scene for the chapters that follow by examining the ways that times of crisis (natural disaster, war, global health emergencies, financial crises) have impacted experiences of, and responses to, violence against women. This research is drawn together to focus on what was already known about the impact of such crises and the extent to which further knowledge on such impacts unfolded during the COVID-19 pandemic. The chapter goes on to consider why the 'stay home, stay safe' government-imposed restrictions, introduced at various times and in diverse ways worldwide, have increased the risk for women and children experiencing domestic and family violence. This chapter considers these issues and their variable impact and interconnections with social inequalities more generally through the lens of social precarity.

Keywords Violence against women · COVID-19 · Crisis · Precarity

INTRODUCTION

The World Health Organisation (WHO) declared the novel coronavirus (hereinafter, COVID-19) a pandemic on 11 March 2020. However, by the end of January 2020, governments across the globe had already begun to enact pandemic control measures. These restrictions varied across the world ranging from communities being placed under total

N. Pfitzner et al., *Violence Against Women During Coronavirus*,
https://doi.org/10.1007/978-3-031-29356-6_1

lockdown (in China for example) to the introduction of less-draconian 'shelter at home'/'stay-at-home' government directives (in the UK and the US for example). From January to June 2020, academics, advocates and media commentators became increasingly focused on the unintended consequences of these required changes in social behaviour, especially for women and children. These concerns were led by Phumzile Mlambo-Ngcuka, Executive Director of United Nations (UN) Women, who in April 2020 stated that confinement would foster tension and strain created by security, health and money worries with increasing isolation for women with violent partners. She described the situation as 'a perfect storm for controlling, violent behaviour behind closed doors', naming the gendered consequences of COVID-19 isolation restrictions 'the shadow pandemic' (UN Women, 2020). This view was endorsed by ActionAid (2020), which declared that the world was 'sleep walking into the shadow pandemic of global femicide'. Thus, the scene was set for COVID-19 to further exacerbate the already existing global problem of violence(s) against women and children. Indeed, throughout the first two years of the pandemic, and to the present day, the safety of women and children has remained an issue of focal concern.

Drawing on a range of empirical evidence, this book provides a focused examination of 'the shadow pandemic', and its impact on women and children across the globe. This chapter begins the investigation by subjecting the concern for the safety of women and children during periods of restrictions throughout the pandemic to critical scrutiny. It sets the wider context in which an appreciation of the nature and extent of the impact of a global pandemic on violence(s) against women and children, alongside service responses to these issues (all of which are covered in more detail in the chapters that follow), might be understood.

THE PRECARITY OF (SOCIAL) LIFE

The COVID-19 pandemic brought to the fore different forms of precarity and emphasised that some lives are more precarious than others. Notably, this was a precarity already experienced as normal and ordinary for the millions of women and children globally who live with the insecurity of violence(s) as a routine feature of their lives (Ndlovu, 2022). This is a life in which each day carries with it the threat of control and the fear of fatal consequences.

The body of work presented by sociologists such as Bauman and Beck have differently focused theoretical attention on precarity and risk, and their everyday consequences. For each of these commentators, their concerns arguably had their origin in extraordinary times (for example the Second World War) and each of them have differently fuelled social scientific concerns with the changing nature of 'modern' life. What each of them might have made of the ongoing and visceral presence of precarity and risk in the second decade of the twenty-first century is moot, but it is nevertheless the case that both precarity and risk have been rendered ordinary for us all. Thus, when these kinds of conditions prevail for everyone—conditions that many women and children routinely manage, resist and survive—a range of questions come to the fore. For example, what happens to understandings of the ordinary experiences of women living with the constant presence of the threat of violence and death (precarity and risk) when this kind of threat is (differently) normalised for everyone? How might these women and children's experiences be understood, measured and responded to during times of global uncertainty? The larger theoretical landscape of the work of Bauman and Beck offers one way to begin to make sense of the different and differential impact of the pandemic on violence(s) against women and children. When placed in a global context, it quickly becomes manifest that such impacts have been, and will continue to be, far from democratic.

In an edited book published in 2021, Didier Fassin and Marion Fourcade brought together an impressive collection of analysis into the consequences of the COVID-19 pandemic on the economy and society globally. As the title of their book implies, the focus of their collection was primarily economic—yet between its pages it is possible to discern the interconnections with the focus of that book and the concerns of this one. In his contribution to the collection, Fassin (2021), points out that rather than the COVID-19 pandemic itself being unprecedented (citing the influenza pandemic of 1918 as one reference point), 'More accurately, it is the response to the pandemic that has been unprecedented, with complete lockdowns implemented in many places across the globe' (Fassin, 2021, p. 155). He goes on to highlight the public health contradictions and tensions underpinning these responses (in particular, the public and policy dilemma over which lives to save) and, in so doing, offers an appreciation of the consequences of lockdowns in the following way:

> These consequences can be seen from two different angles: missing lives and injured lives. The former corresponds to the physical expression of life, the latter to its social expression — the biological and the biographical. In both cases, inequalities are predictable. (Fassin, 2021, p. 169)

Fassin does not make explicit the connections between these consequences and their potential impact on rates of violence(s) against women and children. However, through the analysis of the societal impact of the COVID-19 pandemic offered by Fassin, such observations are there to be made. He goes on to say that the consequences of the pandemic, when viewed through the lens of a moral economy (his term), were, and are, not only raced, aged and so on (having definitive global geographic contours), but also gendered.

In an early systematic review of the potential gendered consequences of the pandemic, Peterman et al. (2020) list nine pathways in which there might be both a direct and indirect impact on violence against women and girls:

1. economic insecurity and poverty-related stress,
2. quarantines and social isolation,
3. disaster and conflict-related unrest and instability,
4. exposure to exploitative relationships due to changing demographics,
5. reduced health service availability and access to first responders,
6. inability of women to temporarily escape abusive partners,
7. virus-specific sources of violence,
8. exposure to violence and coercion in response efforts, and
9. violence perpetrated against health care workers. (Peterman et al., 2020, p. 5)

For Peterman et al. (2020), each of these pathways is gendered and serves to remind us that 'disasters' of all kinds, whether global or more geographically localised—as is often the case with natural disasters—carry gendered consequences, particularly in relation to the violence(s) experienced by women and children.

Contextualising the Impact
of the COVID-19 Pandemic on Violence(s)
Against Women and Children

As the following discussion demonstrates, evidence points to the fact that natural disasters, from tsunamis to earthquakes and bushfires, as well as conflicts of all kinds, have the capacity to add significantly to the toll paid by women and children at the hands of primarily male perpetrators. The gendered consequences of genocide, war and other forms of conflict (in which men are also brutalised) are well documented (see inter alia McGarry & Walklate, 2019; Rafter, 2016). Moreover, work following the 2008 Global Financial Crisis (Bhattacarya, 2013) documented the violent gendered consequences of those economic circumstances echoing the observations made by Hooks (2020, p. 4) on the impact of the Great Depression of 1933, where he observes:

> If you've read accounts of life during the Great Depression, you know that the problem wasn't the valuation of companies but rather a vast and incalculable accumulation of human misery—suicides, starvation, the dissolution of families, violence both domestic and impersonal. (Hooks, 2020, p. 4)

Work in India (Rao, 2020), the Philippines and Vietnam (Nguyen & Rydstrom, 2018), Iran (Sohrabizadeh, 2016), and Japan (Yoshihama et al., 2019) all point to the increase in stresses placed on family life during and immediately following times of disaster. All of which can be connected to increases in the resort to violence(s). For example, after Hurricane Katrina in the US in 2005, researchers reported a 98% increase in physical violence towards women (cited in Morley et al., 2021). Events such as these frequently take their toll on the poorest members of a community on a wide range of dimensions—or, as Peterman et al. (2020) might say, 'pathways'—including economic abuse and violence(s). The consequences of such events are gendered (True, 2013; see also Harville et al., 2011). This 'accumulation of human misery' (to use the words of Hooks, 2020) lends some weight to both the biological and the biographical consequences of precarity outlined by Fassin (2021). Moreover, as Fassin (2021) also suggests, the fact that such consequences are riven with inequalities is, to some extent, predictable.

For example, to focus specifically on violence(s) against women, Lauve-Moon and Ferreira (2017) and Parkinson (2019) have pointed to the ways in which, when disasters happen, the vulnerabilities of those living with violence in their lives become compounded and their needs more complex. This is a finding reiterated by Pfitzner et al. (2020) for women living under lockdown in Australia during the first year of the pandemic. Thus, it is reasonable to conclude that, as Morley et al. (2021) have indicated, disasters disproportionately impact on those already vulnerable, and that impact extends to violence(s). Such inequalities engender slow violence(s) (Wonders, 2018) and can result in 'deaths of despair' (Case & Deaton, 2020). Indeed, evidence from other public health epidemics (like the Ebola and Zika viruses) pointedly indicates that access to health care as well as access to social protection, education and justice becomes problematically compounded for women and children (Fraser, 2020), thus adding to the biological and biographical challenges faced by them: the slow violence(s) of their lives. As Vahedi et al. (2021) argue:

> Reciprocal relationships between infectious disease epidemics and gender-based violence were noted in the Ebola responses in Central and West Africa. Fear of virus transmission acted as a barrier to service seeking related to gender-based violence, and social distancing measures restricted women's and girls' access to safe spaces, reducing opportunities to connect with protective social networks. Communities also reported an increase in sexual and physical violence, sexual abuse and exploitation, child marriage, and trafficking—at the same time that access to services and social support networks are constrained. (Vahedi et al., 2021, p. 8)

In searching for what Vahedi et al. (2021) call a 'syndemic approach', they expose the complex ways in which the slow violence(s) of life interweave and compound one another. Some of this complex interweaving is illustrated in the views of women documented by UN Women (2021a). In a systematic evidenced-based report conducted during the pandemic, UN Women document increased feelings of fearfulness in both public and private places for women (alongside a range of other findings) when pre- and post-COVID-19 views are compared. Thus, the complex way in which 'disasters' impact on everyone's lives, in direct and indirect ways (which do not always include physical violence, as UN Women, 2021a reports), returns us to the issue of the changing nature of precarity for all as intimated above. However, at the same time, the point that such changing circumstances take their greatest biological and biographical toll (Fassin, 2021) on the least powerful (for the purposes of this book: women and children) remains front and centre.

To be clear, none of the evidence cited above or drawn on that follows in this book implies, or is intended to imply, that lockdowns and other similar public health initiatives put in place during a global pandemic are the *cause* of the violence(s) with which this book is concerned. The drivers of male violence against women are well evidenced, and include gender and structural inequalities (Our Watch, 2015). The intention here is to situate public health and other responses to the COVID-19 pandemic within the context of what was, and is, already known about the potential for disasters of all kinds to take their toll in structurally uneven ways across the globe.

In the context of violence(s) against women and children, it is important to remember that the nature and extent of this problem were already featuring on national and international agendas, as illustrated in the UN Strategic Development Goals (SDGs). These goals were set in tune with the available global data which, for example, indicated that during 2017, some 87,000 women and girls worldwide were intentionally killed, with over 50% of those deaths occurring at the hands of a partner or ex-partner (UN Office on Drugs and Crime, 2018). That report concluded that the 'home' remains the most dangerous place for women (and children) worldwide (UN Office on Drugs and Crime, 2018). Findings such as these are repeated year on year—globally and locally—and have remained stubbornly persistent in recent decades. They reflect the fatal tip of the iceberg when it comes to violence(s) against women (and children)—in other words, the number of women and children killed and recorded by such organisations as the UN is limited to those whose deaths were *officially* recorded. It is well documented that male violence against women and children often goes unreported and, consequently, unrecorded. As such the figures stated above are likely underestimations.

It is also important to recognise that male violence against women and children, as has occurred during the COVID-19 pandemic, carries significant economic costs. Again, by way of illustration, Hoeffler and Fearon (2014) estimated that in 2015 alone, intimate partner violence (IPV) cost the global economy in the region of $4.4 trillion a year, or just over 5% of the global GDP. The European Institute of Gender Equality (EIGE) (2021, p. 24) reports 'an estimated cost of EUR 366 billion for gender-based violence (of which 79% is carried out against women) and EUR

175 billion for intimate partner violence (of which 87% is carried out against women)' for the 27 EU countries for 2019. These financial estimates are supported by the World Bank, who in 2019 reported that: 'In some countries, violence against women is estimated to cost countries up to 3.7% of their GDP – more than double what most governments spend on education'.

Yet in plain view of such knowledge and its associated economic costs, throughout the COVID-19 pandemic the home became a central feature of public policy imperatives across the globe. Specifically, the home became a place of safety (away from the virus), while at the same time continuing to represent a place of insecurity (due to violence). This contradiction has been the subject of considerable empirical investigation.

THE GENDERED CONSEQUENCES OF THE PANDEMIC

The impact of stay-at-home directives on the nature and extent of violence(s) experienced, as explored in Chapter 2, represents only part of the COVID-19 gendered consequences story. The rapid gender assessment survey conducted by UN Women and published in 2021 stands as a testimony to the wider impact of the pandemic on women and children, ranging from direct physical violence to food poverty. In the face of such experiences, evidence suggests that around the world many turned to online support (see, for example, UN Women-Women Count, 2021a). A similar systematic review in late 2021 by UN Women-Women Count (2021b) documents the ways in which the consequences of these pandemic experiences result in economic costs for those so impacted, increasing their domestic labour along with an inability to access support services. Indeed, there is widespread documented evidence concerning the impact of lockdowns on the wider delivery of services for women and children, including criminal justice and support services.

In Australia, research by Pfitzner et al. (2020), Carrington et al. (2021) and Women's Safety NSW (2020) pointed to the increasing complexity of needs among women presenting for support to specialist services during the first year of the pandemic—a finding also endorsed by research undertaken in New Zealand (Sibley et al., 2020). With increased calls to helplines documented in a wide range of jurisdictions across the globe, some governments were pressed into providing (at least) additional financial support for those impacted by domestic violence and/or increased funding to support services. For example, on 2 May 2020 the

UK Government announced a £76 million package for domestic abuse charities in recognition of the additional strains they were experiencing.

Increased demands from individuals seeking help also resulted in a wide range of activity among criminal justice services. For example, a new policing taskforce was introduced in Victoria, Australia, called Operation Ribbon. It was designed to provide a proactive focus on policing high-risk domestic violence perpetrators and their victims during lockdown. In England and Wales, Walklate et al. (2021a, 2021b) documented the impact of responding to domestic abuse during the pandemic among 22 different police forces and the associated changes in multi-agency risk assessment conferencing, as many practices moved to online delivery. Initiatives such as this have stretched out into wider, and in some instances new, community initiatives involving the use of pharmacies as safe places in which women are able to report abuse (UK and Europe), and hoteliers making empty accommodation available to women seeking safety from abuse (France).

The nature and effectiveness of this patchwork of responses worldwide is developed further in the chapters that follow in this book. However, to assume access to any of these initiatives was even or equitable would be mistaken. Those women and children all too often already marginalised by service delivery prior to the pandemic (for example, women living with disabilities, children growing up with existing household and parenting stress, domestic workers, migrant women, women from ethnic minorities) continued to be marginalised as the pandemic unfolded—often under worsening conditions with worsening consequences (see inter alia Fassin & Fourcade, 2021; Segrave & Pfitzner, 2020; UN Women-Women Count, 2021b).

Concluding Thoughts

Much has yet to unfold concerning the impact of this global pandemic on the lives of women and children experiencing domestic violence. Evidence from natural disasters and financial crises indicates that there are good grounds for believing that women and children have paid, and will continue to pay, a high price for the unintended consequences of the public health policy directives adopted in response to this pandemic. That price will of course not be uniformly felt. Researchers have pointed to the disproportionate consequences for women whose migration/immigration/work permit status might be fragile (Segrave, 2020) and for others for whom the only way out of life with an abusive partner under these circumstances might be suicide or intentionally making themselves homeless. These women can also comprise of those hardest to reach and support, which poses further questions for wider support services and the responses available to them. Questions also remain over how the police and courts face the ongoing challenge of taking domestic abuse seriously while, at the same time, ensuring they appropriately engage women while keeping the perpetrator in view during a time of heightened invisibility. In the chapters that follow, each issue raised here is examined in more detail.

Chapter 2 offers a more detailed examination of the impact of COVID-19 on domestic and family violence, paying particular attention to what is known and still unknown about the gendered nature of fatal violence: femicide. This chapter documents the uneven nature of this impact to date globally, and sets the scene for the case study approach adopted in some of the chapters that follow. This case study approach is illustrated in the coverage afforded to the experiences of women living with a temporary migrant status during the pandemic in Victoria, Australia, which provides a key focus for Chapter 3. Chapter 3 also demonstrates the relevance of these women's experiences for marginalised women, especially those living as temporary migrants or with temporary visas in other parts of the globe. Their marginalisation was exacerbated during the pandemic, and Chapter 3 offers considerable insight into what the impact of the pandemic looked like—and continues to look—like for them. In Chapter 4, the lens shifts and attention is focused on the relative invisibility of children in the wider discourses surrounding the impact of the pandemic. Children were considered relatively risk free from the virus—the impact of wider public health directives on them (home schooling for example) and their possible increased vulnerability through being at home to exposure to violence was commented on extraordinarily little. This chapter unpacks this relative invisibility and the concerns it raises about the future health and wellbeing for this cohort of children. Chapter 5 builds on the previous chapters by reflecting on how domestic and family violence services responded to the impact of the pandemic. This chapter, again rooted in empirical data gathered in Australia throughout 2020–2021, documents the development and range of innovative practices that service providers operated with during this time. Of course, the Australian experience resonated with policy and practice responses elsewhere across the globe, and these resonances are clearly documented in this chapter. Moving from service delivery to the service providers themselves, Chapter 6 offers a detailed understanding of the impact that working from home had on the service providers themselves as distinct from the service that was offered. Again, utilising data from Australia but contextualised within what is known globally about the toll this period took on these workers, this chapter provides a salutary insight into what might be taken forward from these experiences. Chapter 7, the final substantive chapter, contextualises policing and court responses to domestic and family violence and the innovative practices engendered by criminal justice systems globally against the bigger picture of moves towards digital justice. Moves such as this were incipient prior to the pandemic but gained an impetus because of it. The criminal justice focus of this chapter endorses the problems and possibilities of such justice practices, particularly for those who might have been, and continue to be, made invisible and/or marginalised as the world continues to address the impact of COVID-19. The conclusion reflects on what is known about the impact of COVID-19 on domestic and family violence, plus what is unknown and what is yet to unfold. In reviewing the evidence to date, and the material presented in this book, it is difficult to make any other case for those already marginalised groups in society: COVID-19 has exacerbated their lot and their resultant life experiences.

BIBLIOGRAPHY

ActionAid. (2020, June 23). *Don't cut women's lifelines, warns ActionAid.* https://actionaid.org/news/2020/dont-cut-womens-lifelines-warns-act ionaid

Bhattacarya, T. (2013–2014). *Explaining gender violence in the neoliberal era.* International Socialist Review (Issue No. 91). https://isreview.org/issue/91/ explaining-gender-violence-neoliberal-era/index.html

Carrington, K., Morley, C., Warren, S., Ryan, V., Ball, M., Clarke, J., & Vitis, L. (2021). The impact of COVID-19 pandemic on Australian domestic and family violence services and their clients. *Australian Journal of Social Issues, 56*(4), 539–558. https://doi.org/10.1002/ajs4.183

Case, A., & Deaton, A. (2020). *Deaths of despair and the future of capitalism.* Princeton University Press.

European Institute of Gender Equality (EIGE). (2021, March 5). *The Covid 19 pandemic and intimate partner violence against women in the EU.* https://eige.europa.eu/publications/covid-19-pandemic-and-intimate-partner-violence-against-women-eu

Fassin, D., & Fourcade, M. (Eds.). (2021). *Pandemic exposures: Economy and society in times of coronavirus.* HAU Books.

Fassin, D. (2021). The moral economy of life in the pandemic. In D. Fassin & M. Fourcade (Eds.), *Pandemic exposures: Economy and society in times of coronavirus* (pp. 155–176). HAU Books.

Fraser, E. (2020). *Impact of COVID-19 pandemic on violence against women and girls* (VAWG Helpdesk Research Report No. 284). https://gbvguidelines.org/wp/wp-content/uploads/2020/03/vawg-helpdesk-284-covid-19-and-vawg.pdf

Harville, E. W., Taylor, C. A., Tesfai, H., Xiong, X., & Buekens, P. (2011). Experience of Hurricane Katrina and reported intimate partner violence. *Journal of Interpersonal Violence, 26*(4), 833–845.

Hoeffler, A., & Fearon, J. (2014). *Post-2015 consensus: Conflict and violence assessment.* https://www.copenhagenconsensus.com/publication/post-2015-consensus-conflict-and-violence-assessment-hoeffler-fearon

Hooks, C. (2020, March 24). Dan Patrick to Dan Patrick: Drop Dead. *Texas Monthly.* https://www.texasmonthly.com/news-politics/dan-patrick-coronavirus-tucker-carlson/

Lauve-Moon, K., & Ferreira, R. J. (2017). An exploratory investigation: Post-disaster predictors of intimate partner violence. *Clinical Social Work Journal, 45*(2), 124–135. https://doi.org/10.1007/s10615-015-0572-z

McGarry, R., & Walklate, S. (2019). *A criminology of war?* Palgrave-Macmillan.

Mlambo-Ngcuke, P. (2020, April 6). *Violence against women and girls: The shadow pandemic.* UN Women. https://www.unwomen.org/en/news/stories/2020/4/statement-ed-phumzile-violence-against-women-during-pandemic

Morley, C., Carrington, K., Ryan, V., Warren, S., Clarke, J., Ball, M., & Vitis, L. (2021). Locked down with the perpetrator: The hidden impacts of COVID-19 on domestic and family violence in Australia. *International Journal for Crime, Justice, and Social Democracy, 10*(4), 204–222. https://doi.org/10.5204/ijcjsd.2069

Ndlovu, H. (2022). Entangled battlefields: Challenges of precarity for womxn under COVID-19. *Empowering Women for Gender Equity, 35*(4), 110–116. https://doi.org/10.1080/10130950.2022.2031731

Nguyen, H. T., & Rydstrom, H. (2018). Climate disaster, gender, and violence: Men's infliction of harm upon women in the Philippines and Vietnam. *Women's Studies International Forum, 71,* 56–62. https://doi.org/10.1016/j.wsif.2018.09.001

Our Watch. (2015). *Change the story: A shared framework for the primary prevention of violence against women and their children in Australia.* VicHealth. https://apo.org.au/sites/default/files/resource-files/2015-11/apo-nid58969_19.pdf

Parkinson, D. (2019). Investigating the increase in domestic violence post disaster: An Australian case study. *Journal of Interpersonal Violence, 34*(11), 2333–2362. https://doi.org/10.1177/0886260517696876

Peterman, A., Potts, A., O'Donnell, M., Thompson, K., Shah, N., Oertelt-Prigione, S., & van Gelder, N. (2020). *Pandemics and violence against women and children* (CGD Working Paper 528). Center for Global Development. https://www.cgdev.org/publication/pandemics-and-violence-against-women-and-children

Pfitzner, N., Fitz-Gibbon, K., & True, J. (2020). *Responding to the 'shadow pandemic': Practitioner views on the nature of and responses to violence against women in Victoria, Australia during the COVID-19 restrictions.* Monash Gender and Family Violence Prevention Centre, Monash University.

Rafter, N. (2016). *The crime of all crimes.* New York University Press.

Rao, S. (2020). A natural disaster and intimate partner violence: Evidence over time. *Social Science & Medicine, 247*, 112804. https://doi.org/10.1016/j.socscimed.2020.112804

Segrave, M. (2020, May 27). *The family violence crisis for women on temporary visas.* Women's Agenda. https://womensagenda.com.au/latest/the-family-violence-crisis-for-women-on-temporary-visas/

Segrave, M., & Pfitzner, N. (2020). *Family violence and temporary visa holders during COVID-19.* Monash University. https://doi.org/10.26180/5f6b1218b1435

Sohrabizadeh, S. (2016). A qualitative study of violence against women after the recent disasters of Iran. *Prehospital and Disaster Medicine, 31*(4), 407–412. https://doi.org/10.1017/S1049023X16000431

Sibley, C. G., Greaves, L. G., Satherley, N., Wilson, M. S., Overall, N. C., Lee, C. H. J., Milojev, P., Bulbulia, J., Osborne, D., Milfont, T. L., Houkamau, C. A., Duck, I. M., Vickers-Jones, R., & Barlow, F. K. (2020). Effects of the COVID-19 pandemic and nationwide lockdown on trust, attitudes towards government, and wellbeing. *American Psychologist, 75*(5), 618. https://doi.org/10.1037/amp0000662

True, J. (2013). Gendered violence in natural disasters: Learning from New Orleans, Haiti and Christchurch. *Aotearoa New Zealand Social Work, 25*(2), 78–89.

United Nations Office on Drugs and Crime (UNODC). (2018). *Global study on homicide: Gender-related killing of women and girls.* https://www.unodc.org/documents/data-and-analysis/GSH2018/GSH18_Gender-related_killing_of_women_and_girls.pdf

UN Women. (2020). *The shadow pandemic: Violence against women and girls and COVID-19*. https://www.unwomen.org/en/digital-library/multimedia/2020/4/infographic-covid19-violence-against-women-and-girls

UN Women-Women Count. (2021a). *COVID-19 and violence against women: The evidence behind the talk*. https://data.unwomen.org/publications/covid-19-and-violence-against-women-evidence-behind-talk

UN Women-Women Count. (2021b). *Measuring the shadow pandemic; Violence against women during Covid-19*. https://data.unwomen.org/publications/vaw-rga

Vahedi, L., Anania, J., & Kelly, J. (2021). *Gender-based violence and COVID-19 in fragile settings: A syndemic model* (Special Report No. 501). United States Institute of Peace. www.usip.org

Walklate, S., Godfrey, B., & Richardson, J. (2021a). Changes and continuities in police responses to domestic abuse in England and Wales during the Covid-19 'lockdown.' *Policing and Society, 32*(2), 221–233. https://doi.org/10.1080/10439463.2021.1896514

Walklate, S., Godfrey, B., & Richardson, J. (2021b). Innovating during the pandemic? Policing, domestic abuse and multi-agency risk assessment conferencing (MARACs). *Journal of Adult Protection, 23*(3), 181–190. https://doi.org/10.1108/jap-11-2020-0047

Wonders, N. (2018). Climate change, the production of gendered insecurity and slow intimate partner femicide. In K. Fitz-Gibbon, S. Walklate, J. McCulloch, & J. M. Maher (Eds.), *Intimate partner violence, risk and security* (pp. 34–51). Routledge.

Yoshihama, M., Yunomae, T., Tsuge, A., Ikeda, K., & Masai, R. (2019). Violence against women and children following the 2011 great East Japan disaster: Making the invisible visible through research. *Violence against Women, 25*(7), 862–881. https://doi.org/10.1177/1077801218802642

Women's Safety NSW. (2020). *Impact of COVID-19 on women and children experiencing domestic and family violence and frontline domestic and family violence services*. Summary Report 26 March.

World Bank. (2019). *Gender-based violence (violence against women and girls)*. https://www.worldbank.org/en/topic/socialsustainability/brief/violence-against-women-and-girls

CHAPTER 2

The 'Shadow Pandemic': Domestic and Family Violence During COVID-19

Abstract Since the outset of the COVID-19 pandemic, advocates, policy makers, scholars and media commentators have sought to understand the impact that the global health emergency and associated public health restrictions have had, and will continue to have, on the prevalence of domestic and family violence (DFV) worldwide. For much of 2020, commentary was anticipatory in nature with data emerging towards the end of the first year of the pandemic. However, the picture remains unclear—with some countries reporting increases in prevalence while others report a decline in reporting of violence throughout this period. This chapter examines evidence on what is known quantitively about the impact of the COVID-19 pandemic on experiences of DFV at global and country-specific levels. To do so, it focuses on what is known about the prevalence of domestic family violence and femicide.

Keywords Domestic violence · COVID-19 · Shadow pandemic · Femicide

© The Author(s) 2023
N. Pfitzner et al., *Violence Against Women During Coronavirus*,
https://doi.org/10.1007/978-3-031-29356-6_2

Introduction

The end of January 2020 marked the beginning of widespread social restrictions ranging from communities being placed under government-imposed lockdowns to the introduction of somewhat less-draconian 'shelter at home' and 'stay-at-home' directives. As COVID-19 travelled the world, and new variants emerged, by 2021 the fatigue and stress of living through a global health pandemic had well and truly settled in. From the two-year period beginning in January 2020, academic and media commentators became increasingly focused on the unintended consequences of these required changes in social behaviour. The potential for increases in violence(s) against women and children became an issue of focus, with the concomitant consequences in terms of fatal outcomes being clearly apparent. This chapter presents evidence of what is known about the impact of the COVID-19 pandemic on experiences of DFV globally. To do so, it examines international quantitative data and provides country-specific case studies to examine how women's experiences of violence shifted in prevalence and severity during the pandemic.

The Changing Prevalence of Domestic and Family Violence Throughout the Pandemic

Early evidence of the consequences of stay-at-home directives for women and children during COVID-19 lockdowns were voiced by United Nations (UN) Women. Forecast modelling released in late April 2020 by the UN Population Fund (UNFPA, 2020) predicted that for every three months that lockdowns continued, an additional 15 million cases of domestic violence would occur worldwide. The UN report published in April 2020 indicated that incidents of domestic violence went up by 30% in France since the introduction of the first lockdown on 17 March 2020, while emergency calls for domestic violence went up in Argentina by 25% post-lockdown on 20th March. Cyprus and Singapore logged an increase in helpline calls of 30 and 33%, with similar increases in demands in reports and requests for shelter being reported in Canada, Spain, the UK, the US and Germany.

Similar concerns emerged globally beyond the reporting of the UN. Indeed, early media coverage pointed to an increase in domestic violence reports under lockdown in Hubei province, China, with media reports giving voice to the pressures faced by many non-statutory organisations in meeting the increasing demands for support. This early media reporting was later substantiated by Dai et al. (2021), who examined police service calls from the time of the outset of lockdowns in Hubei. Their research found that the average weekly calls to police in the periods immediately prior to and following a period of lockdowns were substantially higher than previously recorded reporting rates (Dai et al., 2021). Specifically, the study concluded that DFV calls to police had increased by nearly four times compared to pre-pandemic levels (Dai et al., 2021).

Beyond China, similar patterns in increased reporting and prevalence of DFV have been noted by both media commentators and researchers. For example, early data was widely reported in the UK media during the first year of the pandemic from Refuge, a UK women's shelter organisation. Refuge's data showed that on average calls and contacts to the National Domestic Abuse Helpline had increased by 49% for the week commencing 6 April 2020 compared to pre-lockdown (Refuge, 2020). Beyond call rates, research undertaken in Australia with DFV specialist practitioners similarly documented an increase in the prevalence and severity of DFV experienced during the first year of the pandemic (see inter alia Carrington et al., 2021; Foster & Fletcher, 2020; Pfitzner et al., 2020, 2022).

Throughout this period, some researchers examining the impact of the pandemic conducted research directly with women via survey data collection. For example, a Jordanian survey of 687 women found a four-times increase in DFV experienced since the onset of the pandemic (Abuhammad, 2021). Similarly, an online survey of 246 married women conducted in the Kurdistan region of Iraq found 'significant increases' in intimate partner violence, concluding that when compared to pre-lockdown reporting rates, there was an increase in violence between 32 and 38% (Mahmood et al., 2022). Illustrating the significant underreporting of this form of violence, Abuhammad (2021) found that less than half of the women who reported experiences of violence in the study had reported their victimisation to the police. These findings add some nuanced understanding to earlier work that drew on police-recorded data and found notable increases in the use of violence. It is well documented that such official data sets are likely to provide a partial picture of women's experiences of violence in general, and it is fair to assume that such partiality remained the case during the pandemic.

However, data published more recently continues to complete the picture, offering a more robust assessment of the impact of the stay-at-home directives on the prevalence and nature of domestic violence. For example, research by Boxall and Morgan (2021) in Australia found that 3.4% of women who were in a relationship in the 12 months prior to the pandemic reported experiencing physical violence for the first time. For those women who had experienced violence prior to the pandemic, 41.7% reported that their experiences of violence had become more frequent or severe since the start of the pandemic (on this point, see also Peitzmeier et al., 2021). The Australian report by Boxall and Morgan (2021) also goes on to document changes in experiences of sexual violence, economic abuse and other forms of abusive behaviour towards women during the initial period of pandemic-related restrictions across Australia.

A systematic review of 100 papers presenting research on violence against women and children in low- and middle-income countries one year on from the start of the pandemic conducted by Bourgault et al. (2021) shows that 80% of these papers point to an increase in such violence(s). In addition, Bourgault et al. (2021) noted common findings in the risk factors underpinning these increases in prevalence, citing lost income and employment, food insecurity and spousal substance abuse as common risk factors identified among the studies that found an increase in rates of violence against women during this period. In studies where no increase in prevalence was noted, the review found that spousal employment on the part of either party in the marriage, and a higher education level, were identified as protective factors. While this review summarises evidence from research conducted during the first year of the pandemic, the findings about risk and protective factors may well continue to hold relevance as counties continue to move through the pandemic.

THE CHANGING NATURE OF DOMESTIC AND FAMILY VIOLENCE VICTIMISATION AND PERPETRATION

Building on the focus on prevalence, research since the outset of the pandemic has further sought to document the degree to which new forms of DFV have emerged. Specifically, research conducted in Australia by Pfitzner et al. (2020) drew on the professional experience of DFV practitioners to document the ways in which perpetrators exploited the pandemic and related public health restrictions. In the Australian state of Victoria, participants described ways in which abusers weaponised the pandemic to perpetrate new forms of abuse against their intimate partners. For example, one practitioner in that study described perpetrators:

> Demanding women to wash their hands and body excessively to a point [where] women's skin starts to bleed and become badly irritated; spreading a vicious rumour she's got COVID-19 so nobody would come near her or help her; taking children away saying she is likely to have/get COVID-19 and is a risk to children. (Pfitzner et al., 2022, p. 6)

Other practitioners reflected on cases where perpetrators used the threat of infection and government-imposed restrictions to force further controls on their partners' movements, and to gain unwanted access to their homes (Pfitzner et al., 2022, pp. 6–7). Beyond the emergence of new forms of DFV during this early period of the pandemic, government-imposed restrictions throughout the first two years further enhanced conditions where perpetrators could seek to control their victims. The imposition of stay-at-home restrictions, curfews and work-from-home recommendations may have meant that for women in coercively controlling relationships, the degree to which their abusive partners could monitor and control their movements, had never been greater. In many ways, the restrictions imposed—including isolating individuals from family and friends—mirrors many of the behaviours described by Stark (2007) and others in their conceptualisation of coercive control. Recognising the degree to which government-imposed restrictions mimicked the control of an abuser upon a woman's life is paramount to understanding the potential risks that may emerge as restrictions ease internationally. It is critical to understand the extent to which abusers may seek to retain that level of control over their female partners as communities around the world return to a so-called 'pre-COVID-19' level of independence.

The Impact of the Pandemic
on Intimate Partner Femicide

Media outlets worldwide have raised the alarm about the potential impact of the COVID-19 pandemic on the prevalence of intimate partner femicide—the killing of women[1]—since the early days of the pandemic. Since early 2020, conflicting evidence has emerged on the impact of the pandemic on rates of femicide on global, regional and country-specific levels. Predictions made by ActionAid (2020) in the first year of the pandemic about the potential increase of the killing of women have yet to be fully confirmed. This section explores the contested views over the impact that the first two years of the pandemic has had on rates of intimate partner femicide.

At the global level, a UN Office on Drugs and Crime (UNODC) Research Brief published in November 2021 highlighted the ongoing high rate at which women are killed as a result of male violence worldwide:

> Some 47,000 women and girls worldwide were killed by their intimate partners or other family members in 2020. This means that, on average, a woman or girl is killed by someone in her own family every 11 minutes. (UNODC, 2021, p. 3)

Referring to 2020, the report goes on the observe that:

> At the national level, monthly data from 14 countries in various regions show high variability in trends across countries but suggest that, overall, female intimate partner/family-related homicides remained relatively unaffected by the lockdowns in those countries. (UNODC, 2021, p. 20)

At the country level, more conclusive claims on femicide during the first two years of the pandemic have emerged. Research by the World Bank (2022), for example, found that in the initial months of the pandemic the rate of femicide increased by 50% in Panama, 25% in Costa

---

[1] The definition of femicide is contested. According to the EU (2021) 'Femicide's classification differs according to context, but most significantly includes: killing by an intimate partner or family member; honour, dowry and witch-hunting deaths; femicide-suicide; pre- and post-natal excess female mortality; infanticide; and deliberate neglect, rooted in a preference for sons over daughters'.

Rica and 25% in Ecuador. In Canada, leading femicide researcher Myrna Dawson has flagged concern surrounding the increase in femicide over the three years spanning from a pre-COVID-19 period to late 2021 and beyond (as quoted in Carty, 2021). Dawson cites research collected by the Canadian Femicide Observatory for Justice and Accountability (CFOJA) which shows that over this three-year period there had been a steady increase in rates of femicide. Specifically, CFOJA data shows that 92 women and girls were killed in Canada in the first six months of 2021, up from 78 during the same period in 2020 and 60 in 2019 (see further University of Guelph, 2021). In stark contrast, other studies have concluded that the rate of femicide has in fact not increased since the outset of the pandemic. For example, research undertaken by Aebi et al. (2021) analysed monthly femicide data from six Spanish speaking countries—Argentina, Chile, Paraguay, Panama, Mexico and Spain—to demonstrate that when seasonal distribution of femicides in the three years prior to the pandemic are considered, there does not appear to be any difference in the femicide rates of each country.

Additional research points to the increasing complexities in *how* and *what* we measure in our attempts to understand rates of women killed by male violence since the outset of the pandemic. Pointing to the collateral damage of living with violence, researchers have noted the importance of looking beyond documented femicide rates to other relevant criminal justice statistics. For example, Bates et al. (2021, p. 70), in examining data obtained from domestic homicide reviews, suggest: 'So, it is likely that each year there are more suspected victim suicides with a history of domestic abuse than identified by this project and analysis alone'. Of related concern, some countries have observed an increase in suicide rates since the outset of the pandemic (Santoni et al., 2021), with the 2020 data from several countries including the US showing an escalation in suicides among women and adolescent girls. This research points to the need to be more expansive in what we include in our understandings and calculations of femicide during the pandemic (on the need to reimagine the counting of femicide, see also Walkate & Fitz-Gibbon, 2022).

Data Gaps and the Invisibility of Domestic and Family Violence During the Pandemic

Much of the evidence cited above points to increased demands on support services during times when the challenges of stay-at-home directives were at their most acute. Yet in a systematic review of 17 reports on COVID-19 and domestic abuse, Peterman et al. (2020) point to the inherent difficulties in placing too much weight on administrative data, as it was being reported at a time that such directives were in place. Recognising that the underreporting of violence against women is commonplace in a wide range of jurisdictions (the reasons for which are well documented), Peterman et al. (2020) point out that looking at such data on a month-by-month basis reveals little about wider trends over time and/or the accuracy of the data itself. This can produce contradictory findings. For example, of two early studies based in the US, one suggests a 10% increase in calls to the police for domestic abuse largely driven by households with prior calls of such abuse (Leslie & Wilson, 2020). The second study reports a decrease in such calls in the two cities studied (Mohler et al., 2020). In a study based in the US city of Dallas, Piquero et al. (2020) report a short-term spike in reports followed by a decrease in reporting behaviour. Work by Campedelli et al. (2020) indicates no significant change in reported incidents, with Gerell et al. (2020) reporting a decrease in reports of indoor assaults in Sweden. Freeman (2020) also reports no evidence of an increase in recorded incidents of domestic assault on the introduction of social distancing in the Australian state of New South Wales (NSW), including the figures for more serious assaults for which it is suggested police involvement might still be expected. Moreover, the work of Fitzpatrick et al. (2020) has demonstrated reports of child abuse decline (in their study by 65%) when schools are closed. So, when availability of services is added to what might amount to small changes in reporting behaviour (when women are reluctant to report in any event), administrative data over short time periods may offer little reliable insight into the wider picture of events.

CONCLUDING THOUGHTS

This is a shadow pandemic growing during this COVID-19 crisis and a global collective effort is needed to prevent it. The life of women and children moves from their needs to their rights during this pandemic. It is essential to undertake urgent actions to intervene in it. (Wake & Kandula, 2022, p. 1)

As the above quote by Wake and Kandula (2022) captures, there has been significant attention given towards understanding the impacts that the first two years of the COVID-19 pandemic have had on women's experiences of men's intimate partner violence. To date, however, the picture remains somewhat incomplete regarding the impact of periods of lockdowns, and other restrictions, on the prevalence and nature of violence(s) against women and children. As this chapter has shown, the emerging evidence over this two-year period is contradictory and mixed—with some countries reporting increases in women's experiences of DFV while others reported a continuation of similar rates of victimisation to those recorded in the years prior to the pandemic. This is particularly the case for femicide, where sustained media attention throughout the pandemic sought to ignite fears surrounding the increased killing of women. However, as highlighted throughout this chapter, the degree to which these fears have been realised is, as yet, difficult to understand.

The focus on counting and documenting violence against women and children is important but cannot be our sole focus. It is important to also recognise that the COVID-19 pandemic has exacerbated existing gender inequalities (Grown & Bousquet, 2020; International Labour Organisation, 2020; United Nations [UN], 2020). In April 2020, a report produced by the UN noted that the pandemic is 'rapidly unravelling the limited, but precious, progress that the world has made towards gender equality in the past few decades' (Morse & Anderson, 2020). This includes compounding economic inequalities, adversely impacted access to health services including reproductive and maternal health, and heightening challenges associated with unpaid care work (Grown & Bousquet, 2020; UN, 2020). The heightened gender inequalities arising from this crisis create conditions which are known drivers of male violence against women. An understanding of the structural and gender inequalities arising from the pandemic is therefore critical to undertaking a gender-informed, in-depth analysis of the impact of the pandemic on the prevalence and nature of DFV around the world.

BIBLIOGRAPHY

Abuhammad, S. (2021). Violence against Jordanian Women during COVID-19 outbreak. *International Journal of Clinical Practice, 75*(3), e13824. https://doi.org/10.1111/ijcp.13824

ActionAid. (2020, June 23). *Don't cut women's lifelines, warns ActionAid.* https://actionaid.org/news/2020/dont-cut-womens-lifelines-warns-actionaid

Aebi, M. F., Molnar, L., & Baquerizas, F. (2021). Against all odds, femicide did not increase during the first year of the COVID-19 pandemic: Evidence from six Spanish-speaking countries. *Journal of Contemporary Criminal Justice, 37*(4), 615–644. https://doi.org/10.1177/10439862211054237

Bates, L., Hoeger, K., Stoneman, M.-J., & Whitaker, A. (2021). *Vulnerability knowledge and practice programme (VKPP): Domestic homicides and suspected victim suicides during the Covid-19 pandemic 2020–2021.* Home Office. https://assets.publishing.service.gov.uk/government/uploads/system/uploads/attachment_data/file/1013128/Domestic_homicides_and_suspected_victim_suicides_during_the_Covid-19_Pandemic_2020-2021.pdf

Boxall, H., & Morgan, A. (2021). *Intimate partner violence during the COVID-19 pandemic: A survey of women in Australia* (Research report, 03/2021). ANROWS. https://anrowsdev.wpenginepowered.com/wp-content/uploads/2021/10/4AP10-Boxall-Morgan-IPV-During-Covid-ANROWS-RR.1.pdf

Bourgault, S., Peterman, A., & O'Donnell, M. (2021). *Violence against women and children during COVID-19—one year on and 100 papers in.* Center for Global Development. https://www.cgdev.org/publication/violence-against-women-and-children-during-covid-19-one-year-and-100-papers-fourth

Campedelli, G. M., Aziani, A., & Favarin, S. (2020). Exploring the effect of 2019-nCoV containment policies on crime: The case of Los Angeles. *Journal of Criminal Justice, 68*, 101692. https://doi.org/10.31219/osf.io/gcpq8

Carrington, K., Morley, C., Warren, S., Ryan, V., Ball, M., Clarke, J., & Vitis, L. (2021). The impact of covid-19 pandemic on Australian domestic and family violence services and their clients. *The Australian Journal of Social Issues, 56*(4), 539–558.

Carty, M. (2021, November 25). Femicide rates on the rise during COVID-19 pandemic, says Guelph, Ont. Researcher. *Global News.* https://globalnews.ca/news/8402368/femicide-covid-19-pandemic-guelph/

Dai, M., Yiwei Xia, Y., & Han, R. (2021). The impact of lockdown on police service calls during the COVID-19 pandemic in China. *Policing: A Journal of Policy and Practice, 15*(3), 1867–1881. https://doi.org/10.1093/police/paab007

European Union. (2021). *Briefing: Femicide, its causes and recent trends: What do we know?* Directorate-General for External Policies, Policy Department. https://www.europarl.europa.eu/RegData/etudes/BRIE/2021/653 655/EXPO_BRI(2021)653655_EN.pdf

Fitzpatrick, M. D., Benson, C., & Bondurat, S. R. (2020). *Beyond reading, writing, and arithmetic: The role of teachers and schools in reporting child maltreatment* (NBER Working Paper No. 27033). https://www.nber.org/system/files/working_papers/w27033/w27033.pdf

Foster, H., & Fletcher, A. (2020). *Impact of COVID-19 on women and children experiencing domestic and family violence and frontline domestic and family violence services*. Summary Report. Women's Safety NSW.

Freeman, K. (2020). *Monitoring changes in domestic violence in the wake of COVID-19 social isolation measures* (Bureau Brief No. 145). NSW Bureau of Crime Statistics and Research. https://www.bocsar.nsw.gov.au/Documents/BB/2020-Report-Domestic-Violence-in-the-wake-of-COVID-19-BB145.pdf

Gerell, M., Kardell, J., & Kindgren, J. (2020). Minor covid-19 association with crime in Sweden, a ten week follow up. *Crime Science, 9*(1), 1–9. https://doi.org/10.31235/osf.io/w7gka

Grown, C., & Bousquet, F. (2020, July 9). *Gender inequality exacerbates the COVID-19 crisis fragile and conflict-affected settings*. World Bank Blogs. https://blogs.worldbank.org/dev4peace/gender-inequality-exacerbates-covid-19-crisis-fragile-and-conflict-affected-settings

International Labour Organisation (ILO). (2020, May). *The COVID-19 response: Getting gender equality right for a better future for women at work*. International Labour Organisation. https://www.ilo.org/global/docs/WCMS_744374/lang--en/index.htm

Leslie, E., & Wilson, R. (2020). Sheltering in place and domestic violence: Evidence from calls for service during COVID-19. *Journal of Public Economics, 189*, 104241. https://doi.org/10.2139/ssrn.3600646

Mahmood, K. I., Shabu, S. A., M-Amen, K. M., Hussain, S. S., Kako, D. A., Hinchliff, S., & Shabila, N. P. (2022). The impact of COVID-19 related lockdown on the prevalence of spousal violence against women in Kurdistan region of Iraq. *Journal of Interpersonal Violence, 37*(13–14), NP11811–NP11835. https://doi.org/10.1177/0886260521997929

Mohler, G., Bertozzi, A. L., Carter, J., Short, M. B., Sledge, D., Tita, G. E., Uchida, C. D., & Brantingham, P. J. (2020). Impact of social distancing during COVID-19 pandemic on crime in Los Angeles and Indianapolis.

Journal of Criminal Justice, 68, 101692. https://doi.org/10.1016/j.jcrimjus. 2020.101692

Morse, M. M., & Anderson, G. (2020, April 14). *The shadow pandemic: How the COVID-19 crisis is exacerbating gender inequality.* United Nations Foundation. https://unfoundation.org/blog/post/shadow-pandemic-how-covid19-crisis-exacerbating-gender-inequality/

Peitzmeier, S. M., Fedina, L., Ashwell, L., Herrenkohl, T. I., & Tolman, R. (2021). Increases in intimate partner violence during COVID-19: Prevalence and correlates. *Journal of Interpersonal Violence, 37*(21–22), NP20482–NP20512. https://doi.org/10.1177/08862605211052586

Peterman, A., O'Donnell, M., & Palermo, T. (2020). *COVID-19 and violence against women and children what have we learned so far?* Center for Global Development. https://www.cgdev.org/sites/default/files/covid-and-violence-against-women-and-children-what-we-have-learned.pdf

Pfitzner, N., Fitz-Gibbon, K., & True, J. (2020). *Responding to the 'shadow pandemic': Practitioner views on the nature of and responses to violence against women in Victoria, Australia during the COVID-19 restrictions.* Monash University. https://doi.org/10.26180/5ed9d5198497c

Pfitzner, N., Fitz-Gibbon, K., & True, J. (2022). When staying home isn't safe: Australian practitioner experiences of responding to intimate partner violence during COVID-19 restrictions. *Journal of Gender-Based Violence, 1–18.* https://doi.org/10.1332/239868021X16420024310873

Piquero, A. R., Riddell, J. R., Bishopp, S. A., Narvey, C., Reid, J. A., & Piquero, N. L. (2020). Staying home, staying safe? A short-term analysis of COVID-19 on Dallas domestic violence. *American Journal of Criminal Justice, 45,* 601–635. https://doi.org/10.1007/s12103-020-09531-7

Refuge. (2020, June 7). *Written evidence submitted by Refuge (MRS0192) to Home Affairs Committee.* https://committees.parliament.uk/writtenevidence/3055/pdf/

Santoni, S., Ferrari, A., Dangel, W. J., & Syailendrawati, R. (2021, September 10). Women and suicide during COVID-19. *Think Global Health.* https://www.thinkglobalhealth.org/article/women-and-suicide-during-covid-19

Stark, E. (2007). *Coercive control: How men entrap women in personal life.* Oxford University Press.

United Nations. (2020). *Policy brief: The impact of COVID-19 on Women.* https://www.un.org/sites/un2.un.org/files/policy_brief_on_covid_impact_on_women_9_apr_2020_updated.pdf

United Nations Office on Drugs and Crime (UNODC). (2021). *Killings of women and girls by their intimate partner or other family members.* Data Matters 3. https://www.unodc.org/documents/data-and-analysis/statistics/crime/UN_BriefFem_251121.pdf

United Nations Population Fund (UNFPA). (2020). *Impact of the COVID-19 pandemic on family planning and ending gender-based violence, female genital mutilation and child marriage.* Interim Technical Notes. https://www.unfpa.org/resources/impact-covid-19-pandemic-family-planning-and-ending-gender-based-violence-female-genital

University of Guelph. (2021, November 25). Femicide rates on the rise especially during pandemic, says U of G researcher. *Media Release.* https://news.uoguelph.ca/2021/11/femicide-rates-on-the-rise-especially-during-pandemic-says-u-of-g-researcher/

Wake, A. D., & Kandula, U. R. (2022). The global prevalence and its associated factors toward domestic violence against women and children during COVID-19 pandemic—"The shadow pandemic": A review of cross-sectional studies. *Women's Health, 18,* 17455057221095536.

Walkate, S., & Fitz-Gibbon, K. (2022). Re-imagining the measurement of femicide: From 'thin' counts to 'thick' counts. *Current Sociology.* https://doi.org/10.1177/00113921221082698

World Bank. (2022, March 30). *Covid-19 and femicides in Brazil—The impact of social distancing measures, financial constraints, and mitigating policies.* https://www.worldbank.org/en/country/brazil/publication/covid-19-and-femicides-in-brazil

The Plight of Temporary Migrants: The Intersection of Migration Status, Family Violence and Support

Abstract There is a growing body of research showing that migration status can exacerbate the risk of DFV, and that targeted support is required for migrant and refugee women. Given this knowledge, the impact of COVID-19 lockdowns and stay-at-home orders for women holding temporary visas requires specific and focused attention. This chapter explores the differential impact of migration status on women's experiences of DFV during the COVID-19 pandemic, drawing on 100 victim-survivor case files during the national lockdown in Australia in March 2020. This chapter illustrates the importance of paying close attention to the experiences and responses to DFV and the broader treatment of temporary migrants in the COVID-19 context.

Keywords Temporary migrants · Precarity · Help seeking · Migration · Family violence · Borders

INTRODUCTION

While this book focuses on the intersection of DFV with a global pandemic, this chapter illuminates the importance of capturing the complex intersection with broader policy responses amid the first stages of the pandemic. There is an important body of literature, recognising

© The Author(s) 2023

N. Pfitzner et al., *Violence Against Women During Coronavirus*,

https://doi.org/10.1007/978-3-031-29356-6_3

the specificity of migrant and refugee experiences of DFV pre-pandemic that crosses international boundaries, which identifies how—across pre-migration, during migration and post-settlement—experiences can exacerbate both the potential to experience gender-based violence broadly and also DFV specifically (see Abraham, 2000; Anitha & Gill, 2022; Menjíva & Perreira, 2019; Sabri et al., 2020, Segrave, 2021; Vasil, 2023). The early stages of the COVID-19 pandemic, over the course of 2020, drew significant attention to the specificity of temporariness as a structural position that was connected to inequality and risk—across every context, including financial and labour conditions, exposure to the virus and access to health care, and in relation to DFV. In this chapter, these issues are brought together to highlight how the pandemic intensified, in many ways, the specific structural inequity experienced by temporary migrants[1] experiencing DFV via a study of 100 temporary migrant victim-survivor case files in Victoria, Australia. Weaved into these findings is the alignment with other international research that has also focused on the specificity of migrant and refugee experiences of DFV during the COVID-19 pandemic. In understanding and responding to the known risks of increased and intensified DFV in crises, a view to broader social inequality that is sustained by other systems and structures (for example labour, migration, health and welfare systems) must be cast in order to ensure that any effort or commitment to support women's safety enables all women, regardless of migration status, to have access to support and safety.

---

[1] A note on terminology: in the broader literature, there are different terminologies with various points of focus. Some work focuses, for example, on black and ethnic minority communities (for a detailed account of the use of this term, see Anthia & Gill, 2022, p. 474), while others focus on immigrant women (cf Cleaveland & Waslin, 2021; Sabri et al., 2020), on forced migrants (cf. Phillimore et al., 2021), and on specific groups of women within a particular geography (e.g. Asian American and Pacific Island women in the US, Alnas-Smily et al., 2020; Latina immigrants in the US Cleaveland & Waslin, 2021; Rohingya women in Bangladesh, Chowdhury et al., 2022). In this chapter, the broad focus is on migrant and refugee women, a terminology used in Australia (see Segrave et al., 2021), and more specifically temporary non-citizens and/or temporary migrants. Both the latter terms are used interchangeably. However, we use the specific terminology of authors when referring to their work.

Migrant Women, Domestic and Family Violence and Temporary Visa Status

There is significant international evidence that illuminates the importance of specificity in understanding migrant and refugee experiences of DFV. While the terminology varies, there is significant work that captures how women from migrant and refugee backgrounds are disproportionately impacted by DFV in countries of destination (Amanor-Boadu et al., 2012; Sabri et al., 2020; Segrave, 2017, 2021; Vaughan et al., 2015). A major focus in both research and advocacy for migrant and refugee women is the numerous barriers to accessing support, that are at once specific to personal circumstances (for example, proficiency in the main language spoken in the country of destination, social isolation and access to mainstream services) and more critically, as many have argued, a broader reflection of the structural inequality experienced by migrant and refugee women (Abraham, 2000; Erez et al., 2009; Pearce & Sokoloff, 2013; Sabri et al., 2018, 2020). A key concern internationally is the recognition that temporary non-citizens are either at greater risk or, as Vasil (2023) argues, greater precarity, because of their temporary status. This concern is grounded in an intersectional analysis, following the work of Crenshaw (1991), that calls us to attend to how structural barriers reinforce, reproduce and sustain women's inequality. In this case, gender and migration status are key (Anitha et al., 2018; Pearce & Sokoloff, 2013).

Research focused specifically on temporary non-citizen status and DFV has demonstrated how migration systems interact with sustaining conditions within which perpetrators have greater power and leverage over women, and which countries refuse to accept responsibility to ensure the safety of victim-survivors (Barlow & Walklate, 2022; Segrave, 2021; Segrave et al., 2019). While it is not possible to clearly establish that the prevalence of DFV is greater for temporary non-citizens (Vaughan et al., 2015), there is research that points to the prevalence in relation to migrant women. For example, in 2021, the Immigrant Council of Ireland released a report finding that migrant women are increasingly reporting experiences of DFV, with a 12% increase from 2020 to 2021 (np). In another setting, Anitha and Gill (2022, p. 462) noted that data has demonstrated that racially minoritised populations experience higher rates of domestic violence and abuse (DVA) than their white counterparts in England and Wales.

In Australia, a 2020 national survey of migrant and refugee women found that temporary migrants reported proportionately higher levels of DFV compared to the larger group of migrant women in the study (Segrave et al., 2021, p. 9). While not a generalisable study, this study pointed particularly to the key impact of migration-related abuse (Segrave et al., 2021). Within the broad group of temporary migrants, there are also subgroups where visa status is connected to slightly different conditions and impacts. This varies, of course, internationally, but it is recognised that there can be specific structural and administrative issues that impact women differently if, for example, they hold partner visas (Anitha, 2008, 2011; Segrave, 2017) or student visas (Forbes-Mewett & McCulloch, 2016). The type of visa has different impacts, including the support options in the context of DFV. As noted by Vasil (2023) and Segrave et al. (2019, 2021), in Australia the type of temporary visa is important to understanding the specificity of how the migration system operates as a structural barrier. Key researchers have recognised that these complexities around temporary non-citizenship, which impact a subgroup of migrant and refugee women, are reproducing and reinforcing the idea that this group of victim-survivors deserve less as non-members of the society (see Fraser, 2000). Vasil (2023) draws attention to the importance of recognising that the 'politics of immigration control and its intersections with sexism, racism, and neoliberalism' are an important context that lay the ground for sustaining women's precarity (see also Anitha, 2011; Jayasuriya-Illesinghe, 2018). For this chapter, it is important to extend this critique to recognise that it is not just in the context of DFV that temporary non-citizens are structurally disadvantaged, but also in the broader context of labour conditions and welfare support. In the context of the response to COVID-19 in Australia—as elsewhere around the world—the clear demarcation of temporary non-citizens excluded from various support measures was demonstrable, with consequences that have only been seen, to date, to a limited extent.

TEMPORARY MIGRANTS, COVID-19 RESPONSES AND THE KNOWN AND UNKNOWN IMPACT OF POLICY

Within the setting of the COVID-19 pandemic in early 2020, the focus on temporary migrants was sharpened in a range of ways. The first was the global issue of those who were grounded and unable to leave their places of residence and/or places they were visiting with ease, as borders rapidly closed and entry and exit requirements became both limited and extremely bureaucratic. The second concern regards labour conditions. Globally, the response to the pandemic and the domino of shutdowns of industry that occurred across many jurisdictions illuminated the very specific precariousness of migrant workers (see Anner, 2020; Business & Human Rights Resource Centre, 2020). Alongside fears regarding contracts being cancelled and the economic impacts of this felt by migrant workers, were concerns regarding those whose labour was in high demand and who needed to work but would be doing so in conditions that entailed higher risks of infection from COVID-19 (Business & Human Rights Resource Centre, 2020). Rai et al. (2020, pp. 86–87) noted that, in the context of the US:

immigrants… comprise large proportions of essential workers in industries that remain open during the crisis (Chishti & Bolter, 2020; Chishti & Pierce, 2020; Gelatt, 2020). Not only are they among those who work in the grocery stores and pharmacies that have remained open, but they are also among those most critical to the pandemic response… While their representation in essential industries means they must work during the pandemic, immigrants are also less likely to have health insurance (Narea, 2020a; KFF.Org, 2020). Consequently, if they become ill, they may be less likely to get treatment.

For temporary workers, in particular, a major concern during the early days of the pandemic was precarious and casualised labour. In Australia, in March 2020, the nationally imposed lockdown and stay-at-home orders saw all non-essential workers having to either work from home or cease work altogether, as many businesses closed for the duration of the lockdown period. As Berg and Farbenblum (2020) write:

Many temporary visa holders lost their jobs in heavily casualised industries such as hospitality and retail … Australia is home to over 1 million temporary visa holders, most of whom have work rights. The widespread job loss had a devastating financial impact on these temporary migrants, including international students, backpackers, graduates, sponsored workers and refugees, among others. At the same time, many international students who were financially reliant on family found themselves with less or no support due to the financial impact of the pandemic in their home countries. (Berg & Farbenblum, 2020, p. 6)

As Berg and Farbenblum (2020) noted, the impact on temporary migrants was not just their situation in Australia but the situation of their families in other parts of the world, and the significant interconnecting stressors of separation, immobility and financial pressure. The Australian Commonwealth Government, following some pressure, stepped in to support Australian workers with key financial support packages during the first period of lockdowns across Australia for individuals who were without work and for businesses to retain staff who they would otherwise have to let go as a result of business closure (Senate Select Committee on COVID-19, 2020, pp. 74–75). However, temporary migrants were excluded from accessing these support packages. As Berg and Farbenblum (2020, p. 6) note, this put Australia at odds with other nations such as the UK, New Zealand, Canada and Ireland, who included temporary migrants in their subsidy packages. In their survey-based study of more than 6000 temporary visa holders, Berg and Farbenblum (2020, pp. 8–9) found that many temporary migrants suffered significant loss of income and could not meet basic living needs, and that their wellbeing at home and work was significantly compromised.

Within the debate and discussion regarding the impacts of the decision around financial support provisions, there was limited attention paid to the intersection of this refusal to support temporary migrants financially, and the ways this would potentially exacerbate and intensify DFV. In Australia, at the federal level, the two issues of concern around the so-called 'shadow pandemic' and the refusal to provide any support to temporary migrants—leaving them without any financial safety net—were siloed. There was limited public conversation about the ways in which policy decisions to withhold financial support can have deep and serious impacts on the prevalence and severity of DFV, despite the fact that it is well understood that both financial stressors and major disasters (for example floods and fire) impact DFV (see for example First et al., 2017). However, both in Australia and internationally, researchers were concerned with the ways in which pandemic conditions would specifically impact temporary visa holders, and migrant women more broadly. Rai et al. (2020), for example, noted in the background of their study in the US:

Given their unique positionality in the U.S., the intersectional discussion about the impact of this pandemic on immigrants and issues of family violence is salient. The position of some groups of immigrant women is even more precarious due to the increased dependency on their spouse/partner for emotional, economic and immigration-related reasons. (Rai et al., 2020, p. 84)

The research conducted by a range of scholars internationally made clear the importance of a structural analysis to recognise how policy decisions have differential impacts across a population, and the importance of undertaking close analysis of this for future advocacy and preparedness. The next section provides background on the case study that forms the focus of the chapter, bringing into discussion the international research that has also produced important parallel findings on these issues in other jurisdictions.

COVID-19 Lockdowns, Temporary Visa Holders and DFV Specialist Service Provision: A Case Study of Victoria, Australia

In the context of research happening internationally that continues to monitor the ongoing gendered impacts of the pandemic, this chapter now focuses on a study undertaken in the first stage of the pandemic and the first lockdown in Victoria (31 March 2020–2012 May 2020). Following the methodology of a larger study undertaken in 2017 (see Segrave, 2017, 2018, 2021; Segrave et al., 2019), which focused on 300 case files of temporary visa holders accessing a specialist domestic and DFV in Victoria (inTouch Multicultural Centre Against Family Violence), this study undertook a rapid review of case files related to cases that had come forward during the first lockdown in Victoria (Segrave & Pfitzner, 2020). The specific needs of women seeking help from this service were looked at in the study, examining their situations and circumstances and, as much as possible, the way in which COVID-19 was impacting their lives in the context of DFV.[2] The analysis revealed the ways in which COVID-19 conditions intensified the impact of exclusion in many ways for temporary visa holders experiencing DFV.

Temporary Migrants and DFV: Key Findings

Generally, the service involved in the study provide services to around 40% of clients who are temporary migrants (Segrave, 2017). During the period of March 2020, however, 53% of their clients were temporary visa holders, in April 2020 54% and in May 2020 39% (Segrave & Pfitzner, 2020, p. 16). There was no clear pattern or reason for this: while this was benchmarked against the previous year, the time frame was not long enough to monitor any patterns, and the reasons for numbers changing were difficult to interpret both during the COVID-19 pandemic and also before it. There were significant concerns at the time in Australia—as there were internationally—that women generally would be less able to come forward to seek assistance in the context of lockdowns (see Segrave & Pfitzner, 2020). What was revealed was mixed and requires further trend and interview data to interrogate. Many women did seek out help in part because the economic and other impacts of COVID-19 increased the challenges they were experiencing, but the numbers of clients seeking support fluctuated in a way that did not reflect a neat pattern aligned with the COVID-19 period of lockdown.

Of the 100 women in this study, the majority came from India, China, Vietnam, the Philippines, Malaysia, Cambodia, Thailand and Pakistan. Across the group of 100 women, 29 different languages other than English were spoken at home, and proficiency in English varied: 45% required an interpreter when speaking with their case manager. Of the women seeking support, 54% had dependent children. None of the clients in this cohort identified as LGBTQI+. In relation to their visa status, it is important to understand that the type of visa women hold is specifically connected to the available support and resourcing as detailed elsewhere

---

[2] As detailed elsewhere (Segrave, 2017; Segrave et al., 2021), case files are not produced for the purpose of data analysis and in order to undertake this study, all of the experiences in the case file notes were reviewed and documented into a new databased. The case notes vary in detail and length, some contain significant notations over many points of contact, others only had one or two points of contact when clients dropped out of the system or moved on (for more detail, see Segrave & Pfitzner, 2020, pp. 14–15; see also Segrave, 2017).

(Segrave, 2017; Segrave & Pfitzner, 2020; Vasil, 2022). In this study, 33% held a partner visa (Segrave & Pfitzner, 2020, pp. 18–19). Women who hold partner visas and are on a pathway to permanency can potentially apply to Home Affairs (Immigration) to access the family violence provision to still access permanent residency if they can demonstrate that their relationship was genuine and that the relationship broke down due to family violence (Segrave, 2017). Permanent residency allows greater access to welfare and housing support, in particular. For the 66% of women in this study holding other kinds of temporary visas, that safety net is unavailable. They are far more restricted in relation to the economic, welfare and housing support available to them.

In relation to perpetrators, there is always limited data available in case file notes. The case files indicated that the majority of perpetrators were male partners, 58% were the current husband of the person seeking help, and in 21% cent of cases they were the divorced or former partner of the client. These numbers are broadly reflective of patterns of DFV (Segrave & Pfitzner, 2020). It is also worth noting that while in 84% of the cases in this study there was one perpetrator, 15% of cases involved two or more perpetrators, most often family-in-law members—specifically parent's in-law. This is important in the context of understanding the familial context of DFV and the patterns and experiences of abuse that temporary visa holders and migrant and refugee women experience (see also Anitha & Gill, 2022).

Experiences of Violence: Key Information Regarding the Presentation and Situations of Help-Seeking Women

Of the 100 women in the study, 63% had been physically hurt by the perpetrator in some way, 92% had experienced controlling behaviours, and 38% had been denied food, a secure place to sleep and live and/or medication. In relation to forms of control, this included eight women being removed from their homes; five women being denied money for food or having perpetrators refuse to pay for essentials, including medical essentials for young babies; five women who had no independent access to the house; and six women who were denied access to medical care (Segrave & Pfitzner, 2020, p. 20). During periods of COVID-19 pandemic restrictions, a concern among advocates and service providers was that women who held temporary visas would be less likely to seek help. As noted above, the picture was mixed. It is important to note that this study was based on 100 cases in the first Victorian lockdown.[3] As Melbourne continued to have long lockdown periods over 2020 and 2021, further analysis of reporting patterns would provide a more comprehensive picture. The 'mixed' picture regarding help-seeking was not unique to this study. Sabri et al. (2020) report in their multi-state study in the US similarly mixed responses regarding the amount of calls coming in, with some participants reporting an increase in calls, while others reported a decrease. Both increases and decreases were attributed to an increase in IPV (Sabri et al., 2020, p. 1302).

In this study, a third of the women were separated at the time of contact, so there are longer term consequences that remain to be seen—particularly regarding women who remained in or returned to relationships that were abusive because of financial or other pressures. What was clear was that women who did return to perpetrators, and who were being supported by this service, consistently noted that the reason they returned was the absence of alternative housing, lack of money and the absence of enough government or other support. This was seen to be exacerbated in context of the COVID-19 pandemic. Importantly, findings around the broad situations of risk and experiences of violence and abuse were not dissimilar to pre-COVID contexts. However, there were specific impacts and pressure points clearly connected to or intensified by pandemic conditions broadly.

In some of the case files, specific notes were made regarding how the pandemic and lockdown impacted women seeking support. There were specific stress impacts: for example, in one case a client was scared to go out and take her child out because of the fear of contracting COVID-19, while another client was very concerned about finding a job and her financial survival because of the labour impacts during lockdowns. There

---

[3] Victoria went into lockdown from 31 March 2020 to 12 May 2020. Victoria, more specifically Melbourne, was then in lockdown from 9 July 2020 to 27 October 2020; 13 February to 17 February 2021; 28 May 2021 to 10 June 2021; 16 July 2021 to 27 July 2021; 5 August 2021 to 2 October 2020. During the periods of lockdown, the specific conditions changed, but of importance here stay-at-home orders were in place and only essential workers were able to work outside the home. There were limitations on how many hours could be spent outside the house for exercise, and there were also periods of curfew and restrictions on geographical movement.

were consistent notes in case files regarding the high levels of stress experienced by the clients. This included the stress felt by many people globally who were separated from families abroad and also, often, exacerbated by pandemic conditions and the uncertainty of when travel and connection may be restored, and their experiences of abuse and violence (Segrave & Pfitzner, 2020, pp. 21–23). The recognition that life stressors had been intensified in the context of the pandemic were also reflected in findings from two US studies. Sabri et al. (2020) studied immigrant women and service providers in multiple US states, with 45 survivors and 17 service providers. They found:

> [The] impact of COVID-19 on immigrant survivors of IPV [was described by participants as] … a reciprocal and reinforcing relationship between increased life stressors and IPV due to the COVID 19 pandemic and associated response. Together, these interacted to also shape the mental health of survivors. (Sabri et al., 2020, p. 1298)

Financial hardship was, however, consistent. This was connected both to loss of employment and/or the loss of employment of their partner. In the Sabri et al. study, they found that—across multiple US states—most survivors and service providers mentioned the effects of unemployment on the ability to have basic needs met in the family (rent, food and childcare) and husbands losing their jobs and taking out the stress on their wives (Sabri et al., 2020, p. 1299). Similarly, Gillespie et al. (2022), who studied migrant and refugee women in Italy, found that 'socioeconomic insecurity was … worsened by the pandemic's overall impact on employment sectors and its exacerbation of class inequities. This was especially true for migrant and refugee' (Gillespie et al., 2022, p. 9).

In this study, of the 100 cases, 72 clients were experiencing financial difficulties at the time of contact with the service. COVID-19 was not the consistent causal factor for those financial difficulties, however it clearly had heightened or increased the prevalence of financial difficulties for this group of women. Of the 100 clients, 30 women had paid employment outside the home before the pandemic and the impact for those 30 women was mixed: nearly 70% of women who had employment lost their job and 30% had reduced work hours because of COVID-19 (Segrave & Pfitzner, 2020, pp. 34–35). Critically, this group of women was mostly ineligible for JobSeeker and JobKeeper payments as temporary visa holders.[4] The result was that women were more likely to be reliant or dependent upon their perpetrator and/or require significantly more financial and other support from the service, echoing findings from other international studies (Anitha & Gill, 2022; Gillespie et al., 2022; Sabri et al., 2020). For example, in one case a client had lost her job due to the pandemic and had no income or savings. The reason for this was partly connected to the financial abuse of the perpetrator who had been financially exploiting her prior to the pandemic, but the lack of a job meant there was no way out for her in that context. The impact of the pandemic on the financial stability of perpetrators also impacted DFV contexts for clients. Some perpetrators lost their jobs or had reduced income, which had the flow-on impact of increased violence or threats of violence, further compounded by the limitations on women in terms of exiting the family home. These findings regarding financial stressors and the impact of exclusion from support were echoed by Sabri et al. (2020). They pointed to the stressors relating to family members dependent on immigrant women:

> Being undocumented or having a work visa due to job loss and inability to send money to family abroad was an added stress: 'the focus has been on just surviving because it's not just COVID-19 affecting people here. It's affecting people back home. When I'm on un- unemployment, I don't have enough money to send back home' (Service Provider, Age 40, African). A service provider shared the impact of the intersection between immigration status, access to basic needs and gender-based violence: 'Our undocumented clients have to work under the table, especially during the coronavirus. When you look at Maslow's hierarchy of needs ... there's not enough money for food or rent ... or to keep phones. With abuse, the spouse controls the finances' (Service Provider, Age 24, Latina). The same service provider mentioned that undocumented immigrants are unable to avail public benefits such as unemployment and government assistance which contributes to increased financial hardship. (Sabri et al., 2020, p. 1299)

---

[4] JobKeeper was a Commonwealth government subsidy provided to eligible businesses to enable the retention of staff. See more: https://theconversation.com/job keeper-payment-how-will-it-work-who-will-miss-out-and-how-to-get-it-135189. JobSeeker was a Commonwealth government subsidy that was expanded during the first stages of the COVID-19 pandemic. See more: https://theconversation.com/scalable-without-limit-how-the-government-plans-to-get-coronavirus-support-into-our-hands-quickly-134353.

The case file study limitations are evident here, in that while some stressors were noted, the broader impacts were not always captured, nor was it possible to explore them further. What we see, though—in larger scale studies and smaller, richer qualitative studies—is that consistently migrant and refugee women's structural inequality and exclusion was directly connected to their experiences of DFV.

Broader Service Provision Challenges

Importantly, what is also captured in the context of COVID-19 is the way in which service providers stepped into the void of communication and support for temporary visa holders, particularly for migrant and refugee women more broadly. This is examined in detail in Chapter 5. However, in relation to working with migrant women specifically, other research has highlighted the very specific impacts on services working with migrant and refugee women, including but not limited to temporary migrants. For example, Alnas-Smiley et al. (2020) describe the increase in both the type and amount of work being managed by one shelter service in California with crisis calls and support need increasing but funding being less accessible, as they relied on community rather than government support. Similarly, Chowdhury et al. (2022) focus on service provision experiences in Bangladesh supporting Rohingya women, and the impact of deeming gender-based violence services as non-essential and reducing their capacity. Phillimore et al. (2021, p. 2215) examine the effects of COVID-19 on forced migrant SGBV survivors and the organisations supporting them across the UK, Turkey, Tunisia, Sweden and Australia. They note the inconsistent and unreliable responses to different groups of migrant women and to the service trying to support them. Anitha et al. (2022, p. 474) worked with service providers in the UK and found that the impacts on services supporting migrant women not only increased in numbers but 'a greater proportion of women were presenting with complex needs'.

What was clear for the service provider in this study—but also other service providers in Victoria and across Australia—was that the needs of clients were exacerbated: they were more significant, they required more ongoing support and they involved much higher rates of stress. This all had a flow-on impact in relation to the budget and support provided by service providers and the time commitment to each client, plus the impact on the workforce. In this study, the amount of financial support required by and provided to the 100 victim-survivors ranged from $250 to $5720. A total of nearly $102,000 worth of support was provided to this group of women in a short space of time—on average nearly $2000 per person. To put this into context, case managers revealed in this data that clients who normally would have stopped contact with this service returned because they had no other option for financial support. The financial support was a significant increase on what the service was usually able and did provide to clients. It became evident very quickly to the service that the clients were significantly impacted and that their budget needed to be revised. New extraordinary requests were being made. For example, student visa holders requested support to pay their visa fees, as they risked visa cancellation if the fees were unpaid, and they could not work and had no financial support from the government. The service also created an initiative to provide emergency food delivery to those clients who were extremely vulnerable, including temporary visa holders. It is also important to note that the Victorian Government enabled significantly more money to go into the sector at this time, based on the recognition that DFV services would be at the front line of providing more financial support given the broader economic impact of the pandemic. A major challenge at the time was the exacerbation of what was already a significant housing concern for victim-survivors that had been noted previously in the Royal Commission into Family Violence (RCFV) in Victoria. This often meant supporting women to pay bonds and other housing costs to enable them to find safe housing where it was possible, because they had no employment or income security.

Temporariness in the Context of DFV and COVID-19

As noted above, across Australia and internationally there is clear recognition that temporariness and precarity in relation to visa status is incredibly important in understanding the way in which DFV manifests and impacts women. In the context of the COVID-19 pandemic, it was important to attend to how this played out. Critically, in the analysis of these case files much of the data reaffirmed what was already known regarding the need for structural and service reform to enable safety supports and minimise risk for women who hold temporary visas. That temporariness is consistently used as leverage by perpetrators was well evidenced in the data. In this study, 70 of the 100 clients had details in their case note regarding their own assessment of risk. Over three-quarters of those 70 women indicated that they feared harm or death at the hands of their perpetrator, and 20% specifically feared deportation and/or feared being forcibly separated from their Australian citizen child because of the mother's visa status (e.g. where fathers assert that the mother will be deported and the child will remain with him). A third of the women who identified experiencing fear and risk related to their migration status indicated this was a significant issue. In addition to fearing deportation, it is important to understand the impact or context of the fears that are related to that. Over a quarter of the women in this study feared returning to their country of origin and their fears related to, for example, exclusion or shame in the community. Others feared violent outcomes, while others feared destitution (Segrave & Pfitzner, 2020). This is important to highlight because only one-third of the women in this study had a clear potential prospect of accessing a permanent visa, as they were partner visa holders. For the remaining two-thirds, their fears and concerns of returning home were even more powerful leverage for their perpetrators. Yet, in the context of significant fear, this group of women did make contact and seek help. The long-term outcomes cannot be gleaned from this study, but a major question for future research is what happened to women who did not seek help in the context of assessing themselves as at risk of harm or death from their perpetrator. It is clear that the pressures and impact of temporariness pre-dated the pandemic, but the conditions are important because of the very specific impact they had on families, relationships, and the scale and intensity of abuse.

SPECIALIST SERVICE PROVIDERS AS KEY PLAYERS IN COVID-19

A critical aspect of the COVID-19 pandemic has been the role that specialist services have played in relation to pandemic management and broader policy settings. While there was additional financial support provided by the Victorian State Government for specialist support services, it was clear that there these services stepped in to play a critical role in the context of COVID-19 above and beyond specialist service support in the context of DFV. Specialist service providers stepped in to become health advice communicators. Intake case managers were also providing up-to-date, in-language information about the latest government mandates. A significant part of this practice was to translate information and share it with clients when they were undertaking intake, and at any point of communication while they were working with them. They were not the only service providing this level of carefully targeted, easy-to-understand information about changing policy settings.

In Victoria, this was particularly important because the settings kept quickly changing: policy around financial and income support changed at key points, and it became evident that information was not being well-communicated to various groups, particularly where English proficiency was low and where people were less likely to access mainstream news and other services. In Victoria, this was highlighted, for example, in the revelation that the translation of key government communications was months behind, and that it also was not prepared appropriately in relation to having skilled translators support the translation of information (see Dazel, 2020).

Concluding Thoughts

In Anitha and Gill's (2022) study of service providers supporting black and minority ethnic (BME) women experiencing DFV during the pandemic, they noted:

> Women with insecure immigration status have been hardest hit by the pandemic. The practitioners we interviewed reported extra burdens on their services during the pandemic that arose from both the gaps built into the policy as well as adaptive practice by street-level bureaucrats working within the wider DVA sector. In addition, the pandemic has further diminished support options for women with NRPF [no recourse to public funds]. Women's refuges have been operating at capacity because of increased demand due to difficulties involved in rehousing residents. Despite being underfunded and small compared with some of the larger generic providers, 'by and for' services housed a disproportionate number of women with NRPF during the pandemic. (Anitha & Gill, 2022, p. 474)

This work—plus other research focused on immigrant women, COVID-19 and DFV—has illuminated more of the issues raised in this chapter. Further, Phillimore et al. (2021) recently argued that 'the pandemic conditions exacerbated existing stressors particularly for marginalised individuals with no support', and that this, combined with 'the intensified abandonment by the state', increased the risk of physical violence (Phillimore et al., 2021, p. 2218). These observations are echoed in the findings presented above and draw attention to the importance of in situ research, and the value in making the connections to the international consistency of women's structural disempowerment via, in this case, sustaining temporary visa holders in highly precarious positions. Importantly, other researchers have also extended this analysis to consider women's experiences of abuse and violence both within and outside the home. The work of Alnas-Smiley et al. focuses on immigrant Asian and Asian American and Pacific Islander (AAPI) women experiencing intimate partner violence. The impact of restrictions had made their life more difficult, as had increased experience of hate crimes against their community. The authors note: 'These women are facing a predicament of lack of safety at home as well as outside' (Alnas-Smiley et al., 2020, pp. 407–408).

This chapter has illuminated the importance of locating DFV experiences, women's disempowerment and risk, and the challenges for the service sector beyond the specificity of COVID-19 to more widely consider the implications of broader policies and how they have entrenched inequality of temporariness. The difference between women who experience DFV as citizens and those who are temporary is already significant in terms of service support access (financial support, accommodation, health and welfare), but in the context of the COVID-19 pandemic, this was widened by other decisions. This gap needs to be understood as contributing to violence: refusing temporary visa holders support and creating a national response that embeds this structural difference in our policies actually produces conditions that further empower perpetrators. Responses to DFV in the midst of a global pandemic, or any emergency for that matter, cannot be siloed: we can't claim to be concerned about DFV while refusing to financially support temporary visa holders and then fail to understand that the consequence of that for temporary visa holders experiencing DFV is that the conditions for seeking safety are even further away from their reach.

Bibliography

Abraham, M. (2000). *Speaking the unspeakable: Marital violence among South Asian immigrants in the United States.* Rutgers University Press.

Alnas-Smiley, K., Huey, M., Valmores, N., & Moni, S. (2020). Impact of coronavirus on services to survivors of intimate partner violence: A look at my sister's house. *Journal of Asian American Studies, 23*(3), 407–419. https://doi.org/10.1353/jaas.2020.0032

Amanor-Boadu, Y., Messing, J. T., Stith, S. M., Anderson, J. R., O'Sullivan, C. S., & Campbell, J. C. (2012). Immigrant and nonimmigrant women: Factors that predict leaving an abusive relationship. *Violence against Women, 18*(5), 611–633.

Anitha, S. (2008). No recourse, no support: State policy and practice towards South Asian women facing domestic violence in the UK. *British Journal of Social Work, 40*(2), 462–479.

Anitha, S. (2011). Legislating gender inequalities: The nature and patterns of domestic violence experienced by South Asian women with insecure immigration status in the United Kingdom. *Violence against Women, 17*(10), 1260–1285.

Anitha, S., & Gill, A. K. (2022). Domestic violence during the pandemic: 'By and for' frontline practitioners' mediation of practice and policies to support racially minoritised women. *Organization, 29*(3), 460–477. https://doi.org/10.1177/13505084221074039

Anitha, S., Roy, A., & Yalamarty, H. (2018). Gender, migration, and exclusionary citizenship regimes: Conceptualizing transnational abandonment of wives as a form of violence against women. *Violence against Women, 24*(7), 747–774.

Anner, M. (2020). *Abandoned? The impact of Covid-19 on workers and businesses at the bottom of global garment supply chains.* Center for Global Workers' Rights (CGWR) Research report. PDF: https://www.workersrights.org/wp-content/uploads/2020/03/Abandoned-Penn-State-WRC-Report-March-27-2020.pdf

Barlow, C., & Walklate, S. (2022). *Coercive control.* Routledge.

Berg, L., & Farbenblum, B. (2020). *As if we weren't humans: The abandonment of temporary migrants in Australia during COVID-19 (MWJI, 2020).*

Business and Human Rights Resource Centre. (2020, March 24). CSOS call on governments brands suppliers to urgently mitigate health economic impacts on 60 million garment workers bearing brunt of covid-19 crisis. https://www.business-humanrights.org/en/latest-news/csos-call-on-govts-brands-suppliers-to-urgently-mitigate-health-economic-impacts-on-60-million-garment-workers-bearing-brunt-of-covid-19-crisis/

Chowdhury, S. A., McHale, T., Green, L., Mishori, R., Pan, C., & Fredricks, I. (2022). Health professionals' perspectives on the impact of COVID-19 on sexual and gender-based violence (SGBV) and SGBV services in Rohingya refugee communities in Bangladesh. *BMC Health Services Research, 22*(1), 1–12. https://doi.org/10.1186/s12913-022-08122-y

Cleaveland, C., & Waslin, M. (2021). COVID-19: Threat and vulnerability among Latina immigrants. *Affilia, 36*(3), 272–281. https://doi.org/10.1177/0886109920985232

Crenshaw, K. (1991). Mapping the margins: Intersectionality, identity politics, and violence against women of color. *Stanford Law Review, 43*(6), 1241–1299.

Dazel, S. (2020, August 13). Government coronavirus messages left 'nonsensical' after being translated into other languages. *ABC Online.* https://www.abc.net.au/news/2020-08-13/coronavirus-messages-translated-to-nonsense-in-other-languages/12550520

Erez, E., Adelman, M., & Gregory, C. (2009). Intersections of immigration and domestic violence: Voices of battered immigrant women. *Feminist Criminology, 4*(1), 32–56.

First, J. M., First, N. L., & Houston, J. B. (2017). Intimate partner violence and disasters: A framework for empowering women experiencing violence in disaster settings. *Affilia, 32*(3), 390–403.

Forbes-Mewett, H., & McCulloch, J. (2016). International students and gender-based violence. *Violence against Women, 22*(3), 344–365. https://doi.org/10.1177/1077801215602344

Fraser, N. (2000, May). Rethinking recognition. *New Left Review, 3,* 107–120. https://www.proquest.com/scholarly-journals/rethinking-recognition/docview/1301918978/se-2?accountid=12528

Gillespie, A., Seff, I., Caron, C., Maglietti, M. M., Erskine, D., Poulton, C., & Stark, L. (2022). "The pandemic made us stop and think about who we are and what we want:" Using intersectionality to understand migrant and refugee women's experiences of gender-based violence during COVID-19. *BMC Public Health, 22*(1), 1–19. https://doi.org/10.1186/s12889-022-13866-7 https://doi.org/10.2139/ssrn.3709527

Immigrant Council of Ireland. (2021, November 25). *12% increase in number of domestic violence cases experienced by migrant women compared to 2020.* https://www.immigrantcouncil.ie/news/12-increase-number-domestic-violence-cases-experienced-migrant-women-compared-2020

Jayasuriya-Illesinghe, V. (2018). Immigration policies and immigrant women's vulnerability to intimate partner violence in Canada. *Journal of International Migration and Integration, 19*(2), 339–348. https://doi.org/10.1007/s12134-018-0545-5

Menjívar, C., & Perreira, K. M. (2019). Undocumented and unaccompanied: Children of migration in the European Union and the United States. *Journal of Ethnic and Migration Studies, 45*(2), 197–217.

Pearce, S. C., & Sokoloff, N. J. (2013). "This should not be happening in this country": Private-life violence and immigration intersections in a US gateway city. *Sociological Forum, 28*(4), 784–810. https://doi.org/10.1111/socf.12052

Phillimore, J., Pertek, S., Akyuz, S., Hoayda, D., Hourani, J., McKnight, P., Ozcurumez, S., & Taal, S. (2021). "We are forgotten": Forced migration, sexual and gender-based violence, and coronavirus disease-2019. *Violence Against Women, 28*(9), 2204–2230. https://doi.org/10.1177/107780122 11030943

Rai, A., Perkins, N., & Grossman, S. (2020). The effects of COVID-19 on domestic violence and immigrant families. *Greenwich Social Work Review, 2*(1), 84–96. https://doi.org/10.21100/gswr.v1i2.1161

Sabri, B., Hartley, M., Saha, J., Murray, S., Glass, N., & Campbell, J. C. (2020). Effect of COVID-19 pandemic on women's health and safety: A study of immigrant survivors of intimate partner violence. *Health Care for Women International, 41*(11–12), 1294–1312. https://doi.org/10.1080/07399332.2020.1833012

Sabri, B., Nnawulezi, N., Njie-Carr, V., Messing, J., Ward-Lasher, A., Alvarez, C., & Campbell, J. C. (2018). Multilevel risk and protective factors for intimate partner violence among African, Asian and Latina immigrant and refugee women: Perceived needs for safety planning interventions. *Race and Social Problems, 10*(4), 348–365. https://doi.org/10.1007/s12552-018-9247-z

Segrave, M. (2017). *Temporary migration & family violence: An analysis of victimisation, support and vulnerability.* Monash University. http://artson line.monash.edu.au/gender-and-family-violence/files/2017/10/Temporary-migration-and-family-violence_Full-Report-2017.pdf

Segrave, M. (2018). Temporary migration and family violence: The borders of coercive control. In K. Fitz-Gibbon, S. Walklate, J. McCulloch, & J. Maher (Eds.), *Intimate partner violence, risk and security: Securing women's lives in a global world* (pp. 126–141). Routledge.

Segrave, M. (2021). Temporary migration and family violence: How perpetrators weaponise borders. *International Journal for Crime, Justice and Social Democracy, 10*(4), 26–38. https://doi.org/10.5204/ijcjsd.1995

Segrave, M., & Pfitzner, N. (2020). *Family violence and temporary visa holders during COVID-19.* Monash University. https://doi.org/10.26180/5f6b12 18b1435

Segrave, M., Hedwards, B., & Tyas, D. (2019). Family violence and exploitation: Examining the contours of violence and exploitation. In J. Winterdyk & J. Jones (Eds.), *The Palgrave international handbook of human trafficking* (pp. 437–450). Palgrave Macmillan.

Segrave, M., Wickes, R., & Keel, C. (2021). *Migrant and refugee women in Australia: The safety and security survey.* Monash University. https://www.monash.edu/arts/migration-and-inclusion/research/migrant-and-refugee-women-in-australia

Senate Select Committee on COVID-19. (2020). *First Interim Report*. Commonwealth of Australia. https://www.aph.gov.au/Parliamentary_Busi ness/Committees/Senate/COVID-19/COVID19/Interim_Report

Vasil, S. (2023). "I came here and it got worse day-by-day": Examining the intersections between migrant precarity and family violence among women with insecure migration status in Australia. *Violence Against Women*, 1–29. https://journals.sagepub.com/doi/10.1177/10778012231159414

Vaughan, C., Davis, E., Murdolo, A., Chen, J., Murray, L., Block, K., & Warr, D. (2015). *Promoting community-led responses to violence against immigrant and refugee women in metropolitan and regional Australia: The ASPIRE Project: State of knowledge paper*. Australia's National Research Organisation for Women's Safety. https://www.anrows.org.au/publication/promoting-community-led-responses-to-violence-against-immigrant-and-refugee-women-in-metropolitan-and-regional-australia-the-aspire-project-state-of-knowledge-paper/

In the Shadow of COVID-19: The Invisibility of Children's Experiences of Violence in Homes During the Pandemic

Abstract The invisibility of children and their wellbeing during the COVID-19 pandemic became an early issue of global concern. The UN and specialist children's services raised concerns at the outset of the pandemic that children may be the biggest victims of COVID-19 restrictions, due to their exacerbated vulnerability and invisibility associated with added household stressors and wide-ranging closures of education and childcare settings. Despite this, globally the policy discourse around violence in the home and the role of pandemic-related restrictions in increased risk and decreased detection remained overwhelmingly adult-focused. This chapter explores children's experiences and their invisibility throughout the first two years of the pandemic. Emerging evidence highlights the critical need to ensure attention is paid to children's experiences of violence in the home during the pandemic, and to their related recovery needs going forward.

Keywords Children and young people · Family violence · Invisibility · Harm · Recovery

N. Pfitzner et al., *Violence Against Women During Coronavirus*,
https://doi.org/10.1007/978-3-031-29356-6_4

Introduction

This chapter builds on the broader impact of the pandemic and related household and community restrictions on women's experiences of DFV and associated safety concerns and support mechanisms discussed in earlier chapters. An extensive body of research has identified an increase in DFV during the COVID-19 pandemic (Bourgault et al., 2021; Kourti et al., 2021). With the majority of women affected by DFV reporting having dependent children in their care at the time of the abuse, in DFV research more broadly the increase in women's experiences of DFV during the pandemic therefore equally translates into an increase in experiences of children (Boxall & Morgan, 2021; Carrington et al., 2021; Donagh, 2020; Gibson, 2020; Women's Aid, 2020). Another matter of grave concern was the predicted increase in other forms of child maltreatment, including abuse and neglect (Bullinger et al., 2021; Ghosh et al., 2020). In March 2020, the American Academy of Paediatrics raised concerns about the impact of pandemic-related restrictions on parental and household stress, fearing an increase in severe physical abuse of children (American Academy of Paediatrics, 2020, as cited in Bullinger et al., 2021). Since then, multiple studies have documented an increase in child maltreatment associated with the pandemic (Dapic et al., 2020; Kourti et al., 2021; Whelan et al., 2021; Women's Aid, 2020), making many children the dual victims of increased violence in the home.

From the outset of the pandemic, children were not seen as a priority cohort of concern in wider public health discourses. This was in part attributed to them being identified very early on in the pandemic as *low-risk* in relation to the severity of the health impacts if they contracted the COVID-19 virus (Marmor et al., 2021; Masonbrink & Hurley, 2020). However, with a predominant focus across governments on minimising the spread of the virus and the economic implications on governments and various industries, the mitigation of psychosocial implications of the pandemic on vulnerable populations specifically, and the wider population more broadly, emerged only later into the pandemic (Bullinger et al., 2021; Masonbrink & Hurley, 2020). Some have argued that because children were never seen as a high-risk population infection-wise, concerns around their safety and wellbeing were downplayed or overlooked in public policy (Katz & Cohen, 2021; Katz et al., 2022; Marmor et al., 2021). This occurred despite early calls for action to better protect children from an increased risk of physical and emotional harm associated with pandemic restrictions on households (cf. Whelan et al., 2021), and early alerts to children likely being hit the hardest by the pandemic's psychosocial impacts (Ghosh et al., 2020; UN, 2020).

The effects of the pandemic on children have been described as manifold since its onset (Donagh, 2020; Ghosh et al., 2020; UN, 2020). Wider concerns have been raised beyond an increased risk of physical, sexual and emotional harm: social scientists raised concerns early on in the pandemic around the impact of widespread and unparalleled school closures on children's educational progress and attainment, the impact of restricted access to outdoor activities on emotional and physical wellbeing, and an impact on prolonged lockdowns on other daily routines, such as changed sleeping and dietary habits (Ghosh et al., 2020). Ghosh et al. (2020) reiterated early on that, in addition to the immediate effect on different aspects of children's life, the accumulation of these factors contributed to a decline in children's psychosocial wellbeing more generally (Ghosh et al., 2020).

Concerns around children's wellbeing were further compounded by the effects of the restrictions imposed on households and communities, which significantly reduced opportunities for detection of child welfare concerns by third parties, and access to specialist support services for children and young people (Donagh, 2020; Rapp et al., 2021). The combination of increased risk, decreased visibility and reduced availability of relevant support mechanisms has created what many have labelled the 'perfect storm', further exacerbating children's vulnerability (Rapp et al., 2021; Rodriguez et al., 2021; Women's Aid, 2020; UN Women, 2020). With most of the public health attention directed at the spread of COVID-19—which posed a limited risk to children (Ghosh et al., 2020; Katz & Fallon, 2021; Masonbrink & Hurley, 2020)—children's rights to safety as established under the UN Convention on the Rights of the Child dropped off wider public health policy considerations (Dapic et al., 2020; Katz et al., 2022; Marmor et al., 2021). This chapter examines the effects of the pandemic and its related household and community restrictions on children's experiences of DFV and other forms of child maltreatment, along with the impact on children's visibility, access to support and protection, and the implications this raises for future policy and practice responses.

THE INCREASED RISK TOWARDS CHILDREN IN HOMES AFFECTED BY DFV, ABUSE AND NEGLECT

DFV and other forms of child maltreatment were identified as global phenomena of epidemic proportions even before the pandemic (Dapic et al., 2020; Lee et al., 2022; World Health Organization, 2021). The pandemic has intensified a number of factors and conditions that have been associated with an increased risk of DFV, child abuse and neglect. Research reveals that the pandemic has exacerbated the prevalence and intensity of household stressors, including unemployment of at least one parent or carer, related financial hardship, housing stress, parental mental health and/or parental alcohol and other drug consumption (see, for example, Dapic et al., 2020; Marmor et al., 2021; Rapp et al., 2021; Rodriguez et al., 2021; Swedo et al., 2020). A number of studies have directly linked this increase in household and parenting stressors to the observed increase of violence directed at women and/or children in the home (cf. Dapic et al., 2020; Swedo et al., 2020).

Beyond a general increase in DFV noted across studies (cf. Bourgault et al., 2021), some studies have specifically identified an increase in onset, frequency and severity of DFV (cf. Boxall & Morgan, 2021), along with an increase in the nature and extent of child abuse and neglect (Cappa & Jijon, 2021; Rapp et al., 2021; Rodriguez et al., 2021; Sserwanja et al., 2021). While few studies have focused on children's experiences of DFV during the pandemic, research has alerted concerns that where mothers' experiences of DFV have increased, children have been affected even where children have not been the direct target of the abuse (Carrington et al., 2021; Pfitzner et al., 2020b; Women's Aid, 2020). This is in line with wider research on DFV, which recognises that DFV affecting mothers also directly affects their children's safety and wellbeing (Campo, 2015; Fitz-Gibbon et al., 2022a, 2022b; Humphreys et al., 2006; Meyer et al., 2021).

The experiences of increased DFV by children during the pandemic can be manifold. Firstly, children residing in households where the adult abuser resides were affected by their mother's day-to-day experiences of DFV in the home. Here, research has increasingly recognised that children are directly affected by their mothers' experiences of DFV. This may include seeing or hearing the abuse occur, becoming a direct target of the abuse when trying to protect the mother, and/or becoming the target of abuse often in an attempt for the perpetrator to manipulate, threaten, intimidate and control the adult victim (cf. Campo, 2015; Katz, 2016; McTavish et al., 2016; Meyer & Stambe, 2022; Meyer et al., 2021).

In addition to noting children's experiences of increased DFV in households where the adult perpetrator remained present, researchers and advocates have alerted to the risks of pandemic-related restrictions on women and children experiencing ongoing post-separation abuse. Mothers, along with support services, reported an increase in children being withheld by the abusive parent during contact visits, using pandemic-related restrictions as a means of justifying not returning children to the victim-parent or threatening to expose children to the COVID-19 virus during contact visits (Carrington et al., 2021; Pfitzner et al., 2020b; Women's Aid, 2020). While broader research on DFV shows that the withholding of children is a strategic form of post-separation abuse directed at the victim-parent to create concerns about children's whereabouts, along with fears for their safety and wellbeing (Spearman et al., 2022), it can have equally traumatising effects on children who rely on the victim-parent for safety, structure and security. Further, increased time with the abusive parent may increase the risk of harm towards children (Pfitzner et al., 2020b; Stark et al., 2019). pandemic-related restrictions, therefore, raised substantial concerns for mothers and children managing ongoing safety in the context of shared parenting arrangements.

In addition, some research has highlighted the emotional burden placed on children experiencing DFV, exacerbated by the prominent public and media discourse of severe illness, hospitalisations and deaths within the adult population contracting COVID-19. Research on the effects of DFV on children has frequently linked childhood experiences of DFV with adverse mental health outcomes for children, including anxiety disorders (Lourenco et al., 2013). Many children experiencing DFV worry about the safety and wellbeing of the victim-parent (Meyer et al., 2021; Noble-Carr et al., 2017). Research on the effects of the pandemic on children's emotional wellbeing has similarly alerted the substantial risk of adverse mental health outcomes for children (cf. Lee et al., 2022). For many children experiencing DFV during the pandemic, the fear of harm to the victim-parent and the implications this may have for children's carer arrangements—including being placed into the care of the abusive parent—was compounded by government narratives and the dominant media discourse around containing a deadly virus (see, for example, Richardson Foster et al., 2022).

In addition to children's increased experiences of DFV during the pandemic, research has pointed to an increase in other forms of child maltreatment, including abuse and neglect. A 2020 US study by Rodriguez et al. (2021) captured self-reported parent data on parental stress and the use of physical, emotional and verbal abuse towards children, along with emotional neglect. Parents rated their use of these four forms of child maltreatment as higher since the onset of the pandemic and related public health restrictions (Rodriguez et al., 2021). A systematic review by Marmor et al. (2021) further revealed that studies based on parent self-report data showed an increase in child maltreatment risk factors and an increase in child abuse reported by parents who were affected by heightened parental stress during the pandemic.

While other data sources, such as child protection data, initially identified a drop in child maltreatment, a significant body of research has since then alerted to concerns that child protection data presents a flawed picture of child welfare concerns during the pandemic due to the impact of public health restrictions on the detection of risk to children (cf. Bullinger et al., 2021; Kourti et al., 2021; Marmor et al., 2021). The unparalleled closures of schools and childcare settings globally have moved children's experiences of abuse and neglect behind closed doors (Kourti et al., 2021). In the next section, the impact of restrictions on educational settings and other community-based support mechanisms on the visibility of children and the ability to detect the risk of harm are unpacked in more detail.

Increased Invisibility of Children Due to Specific Restrictions/Impact of Restrictions on Children's Visibility

One year into the pandemic, the United Nations International Children's Emergency Fund (UNICEF) estimated that one in seven children had missed at least three-quarters of their in-person classroom learning. For over 168 billion children, schools had been closed completely for the past year (UNICEF, 2021). In many countries, children remained affected by continuous or repeat school closures for the second year of the pandemic (UNICEF, 2022). While interruptions to community life, including education, is not new in the context of health crises or natural disasters (cf. Ghosh et al., 2020), the extent of childcare and school closures related to the COVID-19 pandemic has been unprecedented (Bullinger et al., 2021; UNICEF, 2022).

Aside from the disruption to children and young people's education and related social interactions, school closures have significant implications for the detection of child abuse and neglect. Education providers make up the largest proportion of notifiers reporting child welfare concerns to child protection services in many countries (Bullinger et al., 2021; Kourti et al., 2021). By moving children out of the classroom to, at best, behind a computer screen and, at worst, into a physically and virtually isolated home environment, the risk of harm to children became increasingly invisible (Bullinger et al., 2021; Dapic et al., 2020; Donagh, 2020). While some governments allowed schools to remain open to provide supervision to vulnerable children (cf. UK Government, 2022), this required vulnerable children to be known to the school or a relevant child protection department—unless parents were willing and able to disclose to education providers that they believed they were at an increased risk of harming their children. As a result, schools remained open to known vulnerable children in some jurisdictions and completely closed to all children in others (UNICEF, 2021). In addition to the reduced capacity of educators to identify child welfare concerns, many vulnerable children were likely deprived of the opportunity to utilise their school as a safe space. For many children experiencing DFV or other forms of maltreatment, school constitutes a safe space that offers respite from their experiences within the home. Further, schools offer an opportunity for children and young people to disclose safety concerns with a trusted teacher or other staff member (Thomas et al., 2020).

In addition to school closures, children were affected by repeat and extensive closures of community-based and recreational services throughout the pandemic. For example, the closures of youth centres, community sports and neighbourhood centres disconnected children and young people from access to trusted adults who may have been able to pick up on emerging warning signs, limiting children's opportunities to disclose such experiences in a space where they feel safe (Donagh, 2020; Thomas et al., 2020). Beyond the restricted opportunities for potential notifiers to identify child welfare concerns, child protection practitioners were equally impacted in their ability to assess new child welfare concerns and conduct any ongoing monitoring of risk associated with existing concerns (Swedo et al., 2020).

Beyond education settings, in many countries, child protection services reduced or eliminated face-to-face contact with clients, including home visits, altogether during the height of government restrictions (cf. Swedo et al., 2020). As a result, the identification of risk to children's safety and wellbeing might have been delayed or missed altogether for many children during this period. Some research further alerts to the impact of delays in court proceedings on ensuring or restoring children's safety and wellbeing. Here, research has shown that the effects of pandemic-related restrictions on child protection service delivery, including the progression of relevant court orders or variations, may have affected children and families in different ways. Throughout these periods of restrictions, children at risk of substantial harm may not have been placed in adequate care arrangements with the urgency required, due to limited court sitting hours and related delays in progressing orders. Similarly, children previously identified at risk of harm and removed from parental care may have experienced prolonged alternative care arrangements despite parents having successfully worked towards reunification, equally associated with pandemic-related delays in progressing relevant court proceedings (Pfitzner et al., 2020a).

Another invisible aspect of child welfare concerns during the pandemic arose from closures of child contact centres (also referred to as 'supervised contact centres') (Women's Aid, 2020). As previously mentioned, mothers and children affected by post-separation abuse in the context of shared parenting often experienced added layers of complexity associated with an abuser's strategic misuse of pandemic-related restrictions to manipulate, intimidate and frighten mothers and children. Some research found that during the closures of child contact centres, victim-parents reported being pressured into agreeing to unsupervised contact arrangements between children and the abusive parent, out of fear of being in breach of their shared parenting arrangements (see, for example, Richardson Foster et al., 2022; Women's Aid, 2020). As can be seen from these examples, children affected by violence in the home faced additional risks of victimisation combined with increased invisibility during the pandemic due to the closure of many of the institutions associated or charged with ensuring their safety and wellbeing.

While children's safety, wellbeing and visibility may not have featured as a priority in government responses to the pandemic, many schools were attuned to the increased risks and support needs among their student cohort. Like many other service areas, some education providers pivoted to ensure students remained visible during a time where it was impossible to physically have eyes on them and their potential safety concerns. For example, a systematic review of 32 studies found that in the European context, some schools ensured that their transition to online learning was accompanied by providing additional training to staff to be better equipped to identify and respond to potential child welfare concerns during virtual engagement with students (Kourti et al., 2021). A Spanish study included in this review noted that some schools further shifted to online assemblies rather than online learning only to maintain student visibility and connectedness to the school community (Roca et al., 2020). However, a UK study raised concerns around 'digital poverty', a concept that captures the decreased visibility and engagement of students who do not have access to electronic devices or high-speed internet (Richardson Foster et al., 2022). The (in)visibility of vulnerable children and its implications for protecting children from DFV and other forms of maltreatment therefore remained a grave concern for researchers, practitioners and advocates globally throughout the pandemic.

Increase in Experiences vs Decreased Notifications of DFV and Other Forms of Child Maltreatment

When examining children's experiences of DFV and related harm during the pandemic, it is important to carefully evaluate different data sources. Research has identified a shift in the reporting and identification of child welfare concerns along with the nature of such concerns. When examining the extent of child maltreatment, researchers and policy makers frequently rely on administrative data sources, including child protection records. While such records only identify the prevalence rates of child welfare concerns that have come to the attention of statutory services, they provide a snapshot of the recorded nature and extent of child maltreatment across countries. Early in the pandemic, child protection data revealed an overall drop in notifications (this is examined further in the next section).

While notifications to child protection services immediately dropped with school closures across a number of countries (cf. Bullinger et al., 2021; Dapic et al., 2020; Kourti et al., 2021; Marmor et al., 2021), some research has identified an increase in certain types of notifications, including material and supervisory neglect (cf. Bullinger et al., 2021). Bullinger et al. (2021) link this shift in notifications to the financial impact of pandemic-related restrictions on households and families. While some families lost part or all of their family income—at least temporarily—as the result of pandemic-related un- and under-employment, many who maintained their employment were forced to work from home while simultaneously accommodating children's supervision and educational needs during prolonged periods of school and childcare closures.

Parents who were forced to work from home may, at times, have been required to let children play or study unsupervised, raising concerns of supervisory neglect in some instances. For others, the implications of unemployment included financial hardship and an inability to provide for children's basic needs, including food and clothing (Bullinger et al., 2021). For many vulnerable families relying on school-based programs providing food to meet the nutritional needs of children, school closures further exacerbated the latter scenario (Bullinger et al., 2021; Donagh, 2020). These research findings highlight the detrimental effects of pandemic-related restrictions on parenting and child wellbeing beyond the risk of physical abuse.

As discussed above, early concerns raised by the American Association of Paediatrics—which predicted an increase in child maltreatment associated with the pandemic and its impact on households and families—were not reflected in child protection data. Child protection data from a number of countries, including the UK, Croatia and different US jurisdictions, for example, reflected an overall drop in child maltreatment notifications (Bullinger et al., 2021; Dapic et al., 2020; Kourti et al., 2021). However, research quickly gained traction in interpreting child protection data with greater care and drawing on more nuanced data sources to obtain a better picture of child maltreatment during the pandemic (cf. Dapic et al., 2020; Kourti et al., 2021; Lee et al., 2022; Marmor et al., 2021; Rodriguez et al., 2021). A US study by Bullinger et al. (2021), for example, examined the drop in notifications to child protection services in 159 counties in the state of Georgia with the pandemic-related emergency declaration and found an immediate drop of 58% in notifications post emergency declaration and associated school closures. The study by Bullinger et al. (2021) showed that prior to the pandemic, the majority of notifications originate from education and childcare providers. Following the onset of the pandemic, the data revealed an immediate drop in notifications from education and child-care providers, which accounts for the majority of the overall decline in child protection notifications during this time. In other words, school and childcare closures appeared to have an immediate effect on child protection notifications in this study. Similarly, a systematic review by Kourti et al. (2021) found that while the documented prevalence of DFV increased across countries included in the different studies, studies examining child maltreatment reports to child protection services noted a decline. In line with Bullinger et al.'s argument, this systematic review links the significant drop observed in child maltreatment notifications to pandemic-related school closures and household isolation (Kourti et al., 2021).

With child protection data offering limited capacity to identify the nature and extent of children's experiences of DFV and other forms of child maltreatment during the pandemic, researchers started to draw on other data sources to develop a more comprehensive picture. Research based on social media posts by young people affected by DFV and other forms of child maltreatment, for example, revealed a 94% increase of child abuse disclosures on Twitter and Reddit within the first three months of the pandemic (Babvey et al., 2020). Similarly, research based on helpline data identified an upward trend, with Petrowski et al. (2020) noting a substantial increase in children and adults reporting child welfare concerns to child helplines in some countries. Further, online surveys conducted with interfamilial child sexual abuse specialist practitioners in the US and Israel revealed substantial concerns among practitioners that children had been placed at a heightened risk of interfamilial sexual abuse associated with increased family stressors and decreased visibility of children during periods of pandemic-related restrictions (Tener et al., 2020). An increase in help-seeking for child sexual abuse was also noted in Bullinger et al.'s US-based study (2021).

Finally, US-based research drawing on hospital data revealed an increase in hospital presentations for traumatic injuries associated with physical abuse during the first year of the pandemic (cf. Kovler et al., 2021). While an overall decrease was observed in hospital presentations for child abuse and neglect in some studies (cf. Salt et al., 2021; Swedo et al., 2020), the same studies revealed that the severity of hospital presentations increased, as demonstrated by the higher inpatient hospi-talisation rate observed for children presenting with signs of child abuse and neglect. An American study undertaken by Salt et al. (2021), for example, examined 579 patient encounters six months before and after the onset of pandemic-related school closures to determine changes in presentations for specific types of abuse, including physical, emotional and sexual abuse, plus neglect and other behaviours coded as child maltreatment. The authors observed no significant change in the prevalence of any of the categories, aside from a concerning 85% increase in sexual abuse incidences. This observation aligns with concerns raised by specialist practitioners that pandemic-related restrictions create an increased risk for forms of child maltreatment that are facilitated by social isolation and secrecy, such as child sexual abuse.

Effects on Children's Short- and Long-Term Wellbeing

The adverse effects of DFV and other forms of child maltreatment on children are well established, including an increased risk of poor physical and mental health outcomes, lower educational attainment, unemployment, intergenerational use and/or experiences of violence, and increased risk of criminal justice system contact (Bullinger et al., 2021; Farrell & Zimmerman, 2017; Gartland et al., 2019; Meyer et al., 2021). Increased experiences of violence in the home by children during the pandemic have raised serious concerns for children's short- and long-term physical and mental health outcomes and associated recovery needs (cf. Bullinger et al., 2021; Lee et al., 2022; Pfitzner et al., 2020a; Whelan et al., 2021). Researchers have emphasised that even short experiences of DFV and other forms of child maltreatment can have significant and lasting effects on children's physical, social and emotional development (Dapic et al., 2020), and that children affected by DFV have individual support and recovery needs (Fitz-Gibbon et al., 2022c; Gregory et al., 2020; Meyer et al., 2021).

Researchers have warned that the effects on children are likely only just emerging. Most of the studies examining children's experiences of violence in the home during the pandemic were conducted during the first year of the pandemic. Many conclusions were written at a time when countries believed they were emerging from the pandemic and preparing for post-pandemic recovery (cf. Bryce, 2020). However, for many countries around the world, 2021 was marked by ongoing or repeat restrictions on education and other forms of community engagement. In

March 2021, 23 countries were yet to fully reopen schools (UNICEF, 2022). As a result, many children affected by violence in the home throughout the pandemic had only recently transitioned back into visible life and everyday routines. The full extent of the impact of children's experiences of DFV and other forms of child maltreatment during the pandemic is, therefore, only just emerging, and it is anticipated to create significant implications for future child and youth mental health, child welfare, education and other policies (Lee et al., 2022; Richardson Foster et al., 2022; Whelan et al., 2021).

Decrease in Access to Support for Those Already Identified as Victim-Survivors and Engaged with Services

The increase in children's experiences of violence in the home outlined in this chapter raises critical implications for children's short- and long-term recovery support. However, this comes at a time where the prioritisation of children as victim-survivors in their own right is increasingly reflected in national policies (cf. Fitz-Gibbon et al., 2022a; UK Government, 2021) but not yet reflected in the adequate resourcing of child-centred support and recovery services (Fitz-Gibbon et al., 2022a, 2022c; Meyer et al., 2021). Child-centred recovery services remain scarce and marked by long waitlists. The pandemic has further restricted children's access to already scarce specialist interventions and recovery support, adding to the length of existing waitlists (Richardson Foster et al., 2022; Women's Aid, 2020).

Similar to the impact on other support services discussed earlier in this chapter (e.g. child protection services, child contact centres, community centres and youth hubs), children's specialist counselling and recovery services were heavily affected by pandemic-related restrictions. Many support services for children are available through schools, community centres and other free specialist service models, and thus became unavailable for face-to-face service delivery during the height of restrictions (Donagh, 2020). As a result, service providers had to pivot in their service delivery to remain available for help-seeking families and individuals. For many service providers, this involved shifting face-to-face service delivery to online support, which created both benefits and challenges for workers and service users (see Chapters 5 and 7 for further discussions of this).

With a specific focus on ensuring children's access to support services, online delivery was described as more suitable for older children and more complicated to implement among younger age groups (Pfitzner et al., 2020b; Richardson Foster et al., 2022). Further, online service delivery created additional barriers to help-seeking for 'digitally poor' families (Richardson Foster et al., 2022) who may not have access to relevant technology and/or highspeed internet required to facilitate virtual counselling sessions, for example (Richardson Foster et al., 2022). Researchers and practitioners further noted that online service delivery with children was more successful where children had previously met the worker or counsellor face-to-face and built some rapport. Developing rapport with children and young people during virtual sessions was described as more difficult by practitioners than developing rapport with adult clients (cf. Richardson Foster et al., 2022).

Practitioners also described challenges in engaging older children and children who had previously developed relationships with practitioners (Richardson Foster et al., 2022). Engaging in counselling sessions from the confinement of one's home raises concerns around privacy and related safety. In small or crowded households, children and young people may not have the space to engage in a virtual counselling session without being overheard by other household members. As a result, children and young people may not disclose recent concerns and experiences or may be at risk of further violence where disclosures are being overheard and/or shared by other household members. While service providers who shifted to online support services implemented a range of safety measures to ensure clients are in a safe and private location when participating in virtual support or counselling sessions, safety and privacy has been limited by the impact of household restrictions on families affected by DFV and other forms of child maltreatment.

Concluding Thoughts

In this chapter, the manifold effects of pandemic-related restrictions on children's visibility and related risk of harm have been explored. Many researchers have argued that the risk of harm to children, and related poor physical and emotional health outcomes, were ignored in public policy responses to the pandemic, which predominantly focused on reducing infection rates (Ghosh et al., 2020; Katz & Fallon, 2021; Masonbrink & Hurley, 2020). While public health interventions and pandemic control measures were necessary responses to an unprecedented public health crisis, they came at a significant cost to the safety and wellbeing of many children and families around the world. Risk of physical and emotional harm increased for children already living with DFV and other forms of violence in the home prior to the pandemic. Research also reveals the increased risk of the onset of violence in the home during the pandemic, placing an even larger number of children at risk of harm over the first two years of the pandemic (cf. Boxall & Morgan, 2021). School and child-care closures have been closely associated with the increased invisibility of children to child welfare and community services. As a result, the risk of increased and undetected harm persisted for many children well into 2022, with many countries still maintaining partial or full school closures two years into the pandemic.

A large body of work has now documented the pandemic-related increased risk as well as the actual prevalence of violence affecting children in the home (Bourgault et al., 2021; Kourti et al., 2021; Marmor et al., 2021; Salt et al., 2021) and alerted to the lasting effects of DFV and other forms of child maltreatment experienced by children—even if only for short periods during pandemic-related restrictions (Thomas et al., 2020). This is in line with the vast body of child maltreatment research evidence established prior to the pandemic, which highlights the far-reaching consequences of children's experiences of DFV and other forms of child maltreatment on their social, emotional and physical development. These include an increased risk of chronic disease, anxiety, depression, lower educational attainment, unemployment, early onset substance use, and youth and criminal justice involvement (Campo, 2015; Farrell & Zimmerman, 2017; Fitz-Gibbon et al., 2022b; Gartland et al., 2019).

Of particular concern are the prolonged restrictions that affected many countries. Research conducted early in the pandemic flagged grave concerns for children's short- and long-term wellbeing and articulated implications for the provision of child- and family-centred recovery support. Much of this work was completed during the first year of the pandemic when researchers expected that communities would emerge from the pandemic ready to address its broader impact on community, household and child wellbeing (cf. Bourgault et al., 2021; Carrington et al., 2021; Donagh, 2020; Katz & Fallon, 2021; Masonbrink & Hurley, 2020; Pfitzner et al., 2020b; Swedo et al., 2020). With the pandemic and many of its restrictions continuing throughout 2022, pandemic-related risk has persisted for many children and access to much needed recovery support has been delayed, with many children only recently emerging from pandemic-related restrictions.

The true effects of the pandemic on children who resided in households affected by DFV and other forms of child maltreatment during periods of restrictions are still largely unknown (Katz et al., 2022) and may be far more detrimental than anticipated in early studies conducted in the first year of the pandemic. The documented, ongoing effects of pandemic-related restrictions on children, and the increased risk for DFV and other forms of child maltreatment, raise crucial implications for the availability of child-centred recovery support (Lee et al., 2022; Pfitzner et al., 2020b; Whelan et al., 2021). It is crucial that children are recognised as victims in their own right with their own short- and long-term recovery and support needs. This requires significant investment into the child-centred support service sector (cf. Fitz-Gibbon et al., 2022b) along with investment into the integration of holistic responses to children and their families (cf. Bryce, 2020). Child-centred support and recovery services need to be made widely available, given the vast number of children affected by pandemic-related restrictions, and related household stressors over the past two and a half years.

It will be critical for governments to consider policy responses to future pandemics, natural disasters or other public health crises. Evidence discussed here provides an important tool to guide future policy and practice responses to ensure that the best interests of children and young people are not again left off the agenda. Future responses must recognise the link between community and household restrictions, related household stressors—particularly financial hardship—and its intersection with parental and housing stress, parental mental health and substance use, and the prevalence of DFV and other forms of child maltreatment and associated long-term implications. They must consider the costs and benefits associated with policy and legislative responses to future pandemics or other crises to ensure early mitigation of risk factors affecting child and family safety and wellbeing (Bullinger et al., 2021; Whelan et al., 2021).

BIBLIOGRAPHY

Babvey, P., Capela, F., Cappa, C., Lipizzi, C., Petrowski, N., & Ramirez-Marquez, J. (2020). Using social media data for assessing children's exposure to violence during the COVID-19 pandemic. *Child Abuse & Neglect, 116,* 104747. https://doi.org/10.1016/j.chiabu.2020.104747

Bourgault, S., Peterman, A., & O'Donnell, M. (2021). *Violence against women and children during COVID-19—One year on and 100 papers in.* Center for Global Development. https://www.cgdev.org/publication/violence-against-women-and-children-during-covid-19-one-year-and-100-papers-fourth

Boxall, H., & Morgan, A. (2021). *Intimate partner violence during the COVID-19 pandemic: A survey of women in Australia* (Research report, 03/2021). ANROWS. https://www.anrows.org.au/publication/intimate-partner-violence-during-the-covid-19-pandemic-a-survey-of-women-in-australia/

Bryce, I. (2020). Responding to the accumulation of adverse childhood experiences in the wake of the COVID-19 pandemic: Implications for practice. *Children Australia, 45,* 1–8. https://doi.org/10.1017/cha.2020.27

Bullinger, L. R., Boy, A., Feely, M., Messner, S., Raissian, K., Schneider, W., & Self-Brown, S. (2021). Home, but left alone: Time at home and child abuse and neglect during COVID-19. *Journal of Family Issues.* https://doi.org/10.1177/0192513X211048474

Campo, M. (2015). *Children's exposure to domestic and family violence—Key issues and responses* (CFCA Paper No. 36). Australian Institute for Family Studies. https://aifs.gov.au/resources/policy-and-practice-papers/childrens-exposure-domestic-and-family-violence

Cappa, C., & Jijon, I. (2021). COVID-19 and violence against children: A review of early studies. *Child abuse & neglect, 116*(Pt 2), 105053. https://doi.org/10.1016/j.chiabu.2021.105053

Carrington, K., Morley, C., Warren, S., Ryan, V., Ball, M., Clarke, J., & Vitis, L. (2021). The impact of covid-19 pandemic on australian domestic and family violence services and their clients. *The Australian Journal of Social Issues, 56*(4), 539–558.

Đapić, M., Buljan Flander, G., & Prijatelj, K. (2020). Children behind closed doors due to COVID-19 isolation: Abuse, neglect and domestic violence. *Archives of Psychiatry Research: An International Journal of Psychiatry and Related Sciences, 56*(2), 181–192.

Donagh, B. (2020). From unnoticed to invisible: The impact of COVID-19 on children and young people experiencing domestic violence and abuse. *Child Abuse Review, 29*(4), 387–391.

Farrell, C., & Zimmerman, G. (2017). Does offending intensify as exposure to violence aggregates? Reconsidering the effects of repeat victimization, types of exposure to violence, and poly-victimization on property crime, violent offending, and substance use. *Journal of Criminal Justice, 53,* 25–33.

Fitz-Gibbon, K., Meyer, S., Gelb, K., McGowan, J., Wild, S., Batty, R., Segrave, M., Maher, J. M. M., Pfitzner, N., McCulloch, J., Flynn, A., Wheildon, L., & Thorburn, J. (2022a). *National Plan Stakeholder Consultation: Final Report.* https://doi.org/10.26180/16946884

Fitz-Gibbon, K., Meyer, S., Boxall, H., Maher, J., & Roberts, S. (2022b). Adolescent family violence in Australia: *A national study of prevalence, history of childhood victimisation and impacts (Version 1).* Monash University. https://doi.org/10.26180/20996761.v1

Fitz-Gibbon, K., Reeves, E., Gelb, K., McGowan, J., Segrave, M., & Meyer, S. et al. (2022c). *National Plan Victim-Survivor Advocates Consultation: Final Report.* Monash University. Prepared for the Department of Social Services. https://plan4womenssafety.dss.gov.au/wp-content/uploads/2022/04/national-plan-victim-survivor-advocates-consultation-report.pdf

Gartland, D., Giallo, R., Woolhouse, H., Mensah, F., & Brown, S. J. (2019). Intergenerational impacts of family violence-mothers and children in a large prospective pregnancy cohort study. *Eclinica Medicine, 15,* 51–61.

Ghosh, R., Dubey, M. J., Chatterjee, S., & Dubey, S. (2020). Impact of COVID-19 on children: Special focus on the psychosocial aspect. *Minerva Pediatrica, 72*(3), 226–235.

Gibson, J. (2020). Domestic violence during COVID-19: The GP role. *British Journal of General Practice, 70*(696), 40. https://doi.org/10.3399/bjgp20X710477

Gregory, A., Arai, L., McMillan, H., Howarth, E., & Shaw, A. (2020). Children's experiences and needs in situations of domestic violence: A secondary analysis of qualitative data from adult friends and family members of female survivors. *Health & Social Care in the Community, 28*(2), 602–614.

Humphreys, C., Mullender, A., Thiara, R., & Skamballis, A. (2006). 'Talking to my mum': Developing communication between mothers and children in the aftermath of domestic violence. *Journal of Social Work, 6*(1), 53–63. https://doi.org/10.1177/1468017306062223

Katz, E. (2016). Beyond the physical incident model: How children living with domestic violence are harmed by and resist regimes of coercive control. *Child Abuse Review, 25*(1), 46–59.

Katz, C., & Cohen, N. (2021). Invisible children and non-essential workers: Child protection during COVID-19 in Israel according to policy documents and media coverage. *Child Abuse & Neglect, 116,* 104770. https://doi.org/10.1016/j.chiabu.2020.104770

Katz, C., & Fallon, B. (2021). Protecting children from maltreatment during COVID-19: Struggling to see children and their families through the lockdowns. *Child Abuse & Neglect, 116,* 105084. https://doi.org/10.1016/j.chiabu.2021.105084

Katz, I., Priolo-Filho, S., Katz, C., Andresen, S., Bérubé, A., Cohen, N., & Yamaoka, Y. (2022). One year into COVID-19: What have we learned about child maltreatment reports and child protective service responses? *Child Abuse & Neglect, 130*, 105473.

Kourti, A., Stavridou, A., Panagouli, E., Psaltopoulou, T., Spiliopoulou, C., Tsolia, M., Sergentanis, T. N., & Tsitsika, A. (2021). Domestic violence during the COVID-19 pandemic: A systematic review. *Trauma, Violence, & Abuse.* https://doi.org/10.1177/15248380211038690

Kovler, M. L., Ziegfeld, S., Ryan, L. M., Goldstein, M. A., Gardner, R., Garcia, A. V., & Nasr, I. W. (2021). Increased proportion of physical child abuse injuries at a level I pediatric trauma center during the Covid-19 pandemic. *Child Abuse and Neglect, 116*, 104756. https://doi.org/10.1016/j.chiabu.2020.104756

Lee, S. J., Ward, K. P., Lee, J. Y., & Rodriguez, C. M. (2022). Parental social isolation and child maltreatment risk during the covid-19 pandemic. *Journal of Family Violence, 37*(5), 813–824.

Lourenco, L., Baptista, M., Senra, L., Adriana, A., Basilio, C., & Bhona, F. (2013). Consequences of exposure to domestic violence for children: A systematic review of the literature. *Paidéia (ribeirão Preto), 23*(55), 263–271.

Marmor, A., Cohen, N., & Katz, C. (2021). Child maltreatment during COVID-19: Key conclusions and future directions based on a systematic literature review. *Trauma, Violence, & Abuse.* https://doi.org/10.1177/152483802 11043818

Masonbrink, A. R., & Hurley, E. (2020). Advocating for children during the COVID-19 school closures. *Pediatrics, 146*(3). https://doi.org/10.1542/peds.2020-1440

McTavish, J., MacGregor, J., Wathen, N., & MacMillan, H. (2016). Children's exposure to intimate partner violence: An overview. *International Review of Psychiatry, 28*(5), 504–518.

Meyer, S., & Stambe, R. M. (2022). Mothering in the context of violence: Indigenous and non-indigenous mothers' experiences in regional settings in Australia. *Journal of Interpersonal Violence, 37*, 9–10. NP7958-NP7983. https://doi.org/10.1177/0886260520975818

Meyer, S., Reeves, E., & Fitz-Gibbon, K. (2021). The intergenerational transmission of family violence: Mothers' perceptions of children's experiences and use of violence in the home. *Child & Family Social Work, 26*(3), 476–484. https://doi.org/10.1111/cfs.12830

Noble-Carr, D., McArthur, M., & Moore, T. (2017). Children's experiences of domestic and family violence: Findings from a meta-synthesis. *Child and Family Social Work, 25*(1), 182–191. https://doi.org/10.1111/cfs.12645

Petrowski, N., Cappa, C., Pereira, A., Mason, H., & Daban, R. A. (2020). Violence against children during COVID-19: Assessing and understanding change in use of helplines. *Child Abuse & Neglect, 116*, 104757. https://doi.org/10.1016/j.chiabu.2020.104757

Pfitzner, N., Fitz-Gibbon, K., & True, J. (2020a). *Responding to the 'shadow pandemic': Practitioner views on the nature of and responses to violence against women in Victoria, Australia during the COVID-19 restrictions.* Monash University. https://doi.org/10.26180/5ed9d5198497c

Pfitzner, N., Fitz-Gibbon, K., Meyer, S., & True, J. (2020b). *Responding to Queensland's 'shadow pandemic' during the period of COVID-19 restrictions: Practitioner views on the nature of and responses to violence against women.* Monash University. https://research.monash.edu/en/publications/responding-to-queenslands-shadow-pandemic-during-the-period-of-co/publications/

Rapp, A., Fall, G., Radomsky, A. C., & Santarossa, S. (2021). Child maltreatment during the COVID-19 pandemic: A systematic rapid review. *Pediatric Clinics, 68*(5), 991–1009.

Richardson Foster, H., Bracewell, K., Farrelly, N., Barter, C., Chantler, K., Howarth, E., & Stanley, N. (2022). Experience of specialist DVA provision under COVID-19: Listening to service user voices to shape future practice. *Journal of Gender-Based Violence, 6*(3), 409–425. https://doi.org/10.1332/239868021X16442400262389

Roca, E., Melgar, P., Gairal-Casadó, R., & Pulido-Rodríguez, M. A. (2020). Schools that "open doors" to prevent child abuse in confinement by COVID-19. *Sustainability, 12*(11), 4685.

Rodriguez, C. M., Lee, S. J., Ward, K. P., & Pu, D. F. (2021). The perfect storm: Hidden risk of child maltreatment during the Covid-19 pandemic. *Child Maltreatment, 26*(2), 139–151.

Salt, E., Wiggins, A. T., Cooper, G. L., Benner, K., Adkins, B. W., Hazelbaker, K., & Rayens, M. K. (2021). A comparison of child abuse and neglect encounters before and after school closings due to SARS-Cov-2. *Child Abuse & Neglect, 118*, 105132.

Spearman, K. J., Hardesty, J. L., & Campbell, J. (2022). Post-separation abuse: A concept analysis. *Journal of Advanced Nursing,* 1–22. https://doi.org/10.1111/jan.15310

Sserwanja, Q., Kawuki, J., & Kim, J. H. (2021). Increased child abuse in Uganda amidst COVID-19 pandemic. *Journal of Paediatrics and Child Health, 57*(2), 188–191.

Stark, D., Choplin, J. M., & Wellard, S. (2019). Properly accounting for domestic violence in child custody cases: An evidence-based analysis and reform proposal. *Michigan Journal of Gender & Law, 26*(1), 1–120.

Swedo, E., Idaikkadar, N., Leemis, R., Dias, T., Radhakrishnan, L., Stein, Z., Chen, M., Agathis, N., & Holland, K. (2020). Trends in US emergency department visits related to suspected or confirmed child abuse and neglect among children and adolescents aged< 18 years before and during the COVID-19 pandemic—United States, January 2019–September 2020. *Morbidity and Mortality Weekly Report, 69*(49), 1841.

Tener, D., Marmor, A., Katz, C., Newman, A., Silovsky, J., Shields, J., & Tylor, E. (2020). How does COVID-19 impact intrafamilial child sexual abuse? Comparison analysis of reports by practitioners in Israel and the US. *Child Abuse & Neglect, 116*, 104779. https://doi.org/10.1016/j.chiabu.2020.104779

Thomas, E. Y., Anurudran, A., Robb, K., & Burke, T. F. (2020). Spotlight on child abuse and neglect response in the time of COVID-19. *The Lancet Public Health, 5*(7), e371.

UK Government. (2021). *The Domestic Abuse Act 2021.* https://www.gov.uk/government/publications/domestic-abuse-act-2021

UK Government. (2022). *Children of critical workers and vulnerable children who can access schools or educational settings.* https://www.gov.uk/government/publications/coronavirus-covid-19-maintaining-educational-provision/guidance-for-schools-colleges-and-local-authorities-on-maintaining-educational-provision.

UN Women. (2020). *The shadow pandemic: Violence against women and girls and COVID-19.* https://www.unwomen.org/en/digital-library/multimedia/2020/4/infographic-ccovid19-violence-against-women-and-girls

UNICEF. (2021). *Covid-19 and school closures: One year of education disruption.* https://reliefweb.int/report/world/covid-19-and-school-closures-one-year-education-disruption

UNICEF. (2022). *With 23 countries yet to fully reopen schools, education risks becoming 'greatest divider' as COVID-19 pandemic enters third year.* https://www.unicef.org/press-releases/23-countries-yet-fully-reopen-schools-education-risks-becoming-greatest-divider

United Nations (UN). (2020). *Policy brief: The impact of COVID-19 on children.* https://un.org.au/files/2020/04/Policy-Brief-on-COVID-impact-on-Children-16-April-2020.pdf

Whelan, J., Hartwell, M., Chesher, T., Coffey, S., Hendrix, A. D., Passmore, S. J., Baxter, M. A., den Harder, M., & Greiner, B. (2021). Deviations in criminal filings of child abuse and neglect during COVID-19 from forecasted models: An analysis of the state of Oklahoma, USA. *Child Abuse & Neglect, 116*, 104863.

Women's Aid. (2020). *A perfect storm: The impact of the Covid-19 pandemic on domestic abuse survivors and the services supporting them.* Women's Aid.

World Health Organization. (2021, March 9). Violence against women: Key facts. https://www.who.int/news-room/fact-sheets/detail/violence-against-women

The Pandemic Pivot: DFV Service Innovation and Remote Delivery During COVID-19 Restrictions

Abstract Government-imposed restrictions introduced through the COVID-19 pandemic raised challenges for services providing support to victims of domestic and family violence. The lack of face-to-face services and the constant presence of perpetrators in victim-survivors' homes during periods of stay-at-home restrictions limited specialist practitioners' abilities to respond to DFV, to assess victim risk and to engage in effective safety planning. To counter these service system barriers, front-line and specialist DFV practitioners in many countries developed service innovations and pivoted to deliver support for victim-survivors remotely during periods of restrictions. This chapter considers some case studies of service innovation during the pandemic and reflects on the degree to which these offer lessons for practice beyond the pandemic.

Keywords Help seeking · Service innovation · Service accessibility · Remote service delivery · COVID-19

INTRODUCTION

Times of crisis and disasters are associated with increased DFV and reduced access to related support services (Hozic & True, 2016; Kinnvall & Rydstrom, 2019; Parkinson & Zara, 2013; Peterman et al., 2020; True, 2013; UNICRI, 2015). The COVID-19 pandemic has

N. Pfitzner et al., *Violence Against Women During Coronavirus*,
https://doi.org/10.1007/978-3-031-29356-6_5

been no exception with reports of increased DFV emerging since the first confirmed cases (Bagheri Lankarani et al., 2022; Boxall et al., 2020; Pfitzner et al., 2020a, 2022b; Piquero et al., 2021). Across the globe, pandemic control measures have restricted people's movements, confining victim-survivors to homes with their abusers while simultaneously increasing barriers to help-seeking and service use (Lauve-Moon & Ferreira, 2020; Onyango & Regan, 2020; IASC & GPC, 2020).

Prior to the pandemic, most DFV services worldwide were based on face-to-face models where interactions between service providers and clients occurred almost exclusively in person (Joshi et al., 2021; Lee et al., 2017; Martin et al., 2020). Restrictions introduced to counter the spread of COVID-19, particularly physical distancing and stay-at-home orders, forced DFV services to swiftly transition to remote service delivery models wherever possible. The transition necessitated the use of phones and digital communication technologies, such as video conferencing, chatrooms and instant messaging applications, to deliver services and interventions.

The widescale shift towards digital interfaces in service delivery has reconfigured service delivery with improved access for some previously under-serviced groups and decreased access for other previously well-serviced clients. In many ways, remote service models have removed geographic and logistical barriers long faced by clients living in rural and remote areas and those with mobility disabilities, providing these cohorts with greater access to specialised, tailored services. At the same time, digital literacy and equity have become critical to service access during the pandemic. Lack of access to digital technologies and the internet led to certain groups of service users encountering barriers to access for the first time during the COVID-19 pandemic lockdowns, and amplified existing barriers for others (Joshi et al., 2021; Tarzia et al., 2018). Some population groups have been totally excluded from accessing services during the pandemic because they cannot afford or do not have access to the internet and/or have low levels of digital literacy. The client groups digitally excluded in the transition to remote service delivery during the COVID-19 pandemic are not insignificant. It is estimated that around 40% of the world's population does not have access to the internet (Agence France-Presse in Geneva, 2021). As a result, pandemic control measures employed by governments across the world have created new barriers to service use and reinforced existing disadvantage, with technology adding a new dimension to accessing DFV support services. This chapter explores the strategies DFV service providers have devised to overcome barriers to service use and improve access during the COVID-19 pandemic. It begins with an exploration of access, then goes on to outline an access model that is used as a heuristic throughout the following discussion of examples of service innovations to address the different dimensions of access.

ACCESS TO DFV SERVICES

While studies have identified a range of barriers to DFV service use, disruptions to services during the COVID-19 pandemic have created new barriers and exacerbated existing challenges to service access. In the context of health and social care systems, access is typically conceived of as multiple factors that operate on different dimensions to influence an individual's service use (O'Donnell, 2007; Penchansky & Thomas, 1981; Peters et al., 2008). The categorisation of factors that influence access varies with most researchers identifying four to five dimensions (O'Donnell, 2007; Penchansky & Thomas, 1981; Peters et al., 2008). Over 40 years ago, Penchansky and Thomas (1981) developed one of the earliest models for access defining it as the degree of fit between the client and service provider (Penchansky & Thomas, 1981). For Penchansky and Thomas (1981) access is comprised of five dimensions: affordability, availability, accessibility, accommodation and acceptability (or adequacy). *Affordability* looks at the direct cost to both service providers and clients and centres on the client's perception of the worth of the service relative to the total cost including their ability to pay (Penchansky & Thomas, 1981; Saurman, 2016). *Availability* relates to the timeliness of service provision and whether the service provider has the requisite resources, such as personnel and technology, to meet the volume of service provision required and specific needs of clients and the community served (Penchansky & Thomas, 1981; Saurman, 2016). *Accessibility* refers to geographic accessibility, which considers practical factors such as venue location, proximity to public transport and travel time in determining how easily a client can physically reach the service provider's location (Penchansky & Thomas, 1981; Saurman, 2016). *Accommodation*, or adequacy, relates to operational aspects of service provision, such as hours of operation, client communication, and referral and appointment systems, and whether these attributes align with the client's preferences (Penchansky & Thomas, 1981; Saurman,

2016). Lastly, *acceptability* refers to a client's comfortability with the service provider regarding 'immutable characteristics', such as age, sex, ethnicity and/or religious affiliation of the provider as well as social and cultural concerns (McLaughlin & Wyszewianski, 2002, p. 1441; Penchansky & Thomas, 1981; Saurman, 2016). Service provider preferences relating to client attributes and payment options also come into play here (Penchanksy & Thomas, 1981; Saurman, 2016). Building on Penchanksy and Thomas's model, Saurman (2016) proposes a sixth dimension—*awareness*—arguing that access should be judged on the use of a service by those in need and those who benefit from it rather than service utilisation alone. For Saurman (2016), awareness centres on effective communication and information strategies. This dimension emphasises that services providers should not have an 'if you build it, they will come' attitude towards service users, and need to tailor services to the local context and population. As Saurman explains:

> Awareness is more than knowing that a service exists, it is understanding and using that knowledge. It includes identifying that the service is needed, knowing whom the service is for, what it does, when it is available, where and how to use it, why the service would be used, and preserving that knowledge. (Saurman, 2016, p. 38)

Recent work on service access has echoed Saurman's (2016) call for greater attention to awareness when considering issues of access (Pugh et al., 2019). The following discussion draws on Saurman's modified version of Penchansky and Thomas's model of access (2016). During the COVID-19 pandemic the dimensions of awareness, accessibility and—to a somewhat lesser extent—availability have played a critical role in shaping access to DFV services. Each of these dimensions are explored below.

Increasing Awareness of DFV Services During the COVID-19 Pandemic

As Saurman (2016) notes increasing awareness of services, what they do, who they are for, and why and how people can use them is central to promoting access. The rapid global spread of COVID-19 has seen stay-at-home and social distancing orders enacted worldwide in an attempt to slow the spread of the virus, reduce strain on health care systems and prevent deaths. Under these novel conditions, public awareness around which services remained open, the hours of operation and how to access them has been key to access. In some countries, including Australia, the pandemic triggered unprecedented government investment in the development of awareness-raising strategies aimed at connecting individuals affected by DFV with appropriate support services. These awareness-raising campaigns used a range of media, such as social media, television, radio and print media.

In the UK, the government launched the #YouAreNotAlone campaign in April 2020 as the country entered its first period of lockdown (Lock, 2020; Home Office & The Rt Hon Priti Patel MP, 2020). The campaign was rolled out across social media channels and printed materials were provided to charities and supermarkets (Home Office & The Rt Hon Priti Patel MP, 2020). This awareness-raising campaign targeted people at risk of or experiencing domestic abuse, and aimed to reassure them that police and special support services were available to help during the lockdown. A social media hashtag campaign was integrated into the communication strategy that aimed to build public awareness and engage people by encouraging them to upload a photo of their hand with a heart drawn on the palm of their hand along with '#YouAreNotAlone' to their social media accounts (Home Office & The Rt Hon Priti Patel MP, 2020). The campaign material linked to a government website that provides information about recognising domestic abuse, help-seeking options, legal assistance and support for people concerned about their own behaviour (Home Office & The Rt Hon Priti Patel MP, 2020; Lock, 2020). The website also provides translated materials and tailored support for people with disabilities. A similar campaign was developed in China using the hashtag #AntiDomesticViolenceDuringEpidemic (International Planned Parenthood Federation, 2020; Owen, 2020).

In Victoria, Australia, one specialist DFV support service implemented a public awareness-raising strategy that involved a shop-a-docket campaign in which contact numbers for support services were printed on the back of supermarket receipts (Pfitzner et al., 2020a, 2020b). The ability of this campaign to discreetly facilitate access to support was crucial at the time. This campaign was rolled out in 2020 during a period of state-wide lockdown where residents were confined to their homes leaving victim-survivors little escape and/or privacy from abusers. At the time, people were only permitted to leave their homes for four reasons: shopping for food and necessary goods, providing care, exercising, and work or education that individuals were unable to do from home. A nightly curfew was in place between 8 p.m. and 5 a.m. There was a one-hour time limit on daily exercise, and people could not travel beyond a five kilometre radius from their homes. Household shopping was also restricted to one person per household per day. Given the gendered nature of household work including grocery shopping, the specialist DFV service specifically designed the shop-a-docket campaign to reach women during the permitted daily food shop. Targeting this rare time outside of the home to build awareness of available local support services provided the opportunity for individuals to seek support while they were away from their abusers. The ability for victim-survivors to seek assistance without perpetrators becoming aware was identified as critical during the Victorian lockdowns as stay-at-home orders increased the presence of perpetrators in homes and limited victim-survivors' abilities to have confidential and frank conversations with service providers and support persons.

Increasing awareness of available services was the first step in facilitating access to support during the COVID-19 lockdowns. The next was overcoming disruptions to the operation of services often deemed 'non-essential' by governments along with the substantial restrictions on people's movements during lockdowns, which inhibited service users' access to facilities. The following section explores strategies developed by DFV services to address these accessibility issues and how they transitioned from face-to-face to remote service delivery models to provide support during lockdowns.

Accommodation: COVID-19 Codewords and Covert Signals

With no guarantee of privacy and confidentiality in homes during lockdowns, many service providers established alternative access points to traditional telephone helplines for individuals seeking DFV support during these periods. These new access channels often involved alert systems where individuals use codewords in text, telephone and online communication as well as signals to access support (Pfitzner et al., 2022b). The use of covert signals to seek DFV assistance is aimed at enabling victim-survivors to let people know that they are experiencing or are at risk of harm without alerting their abusers.

In Spain, the Canary Islands Institute for Equality created the Mask-19 help-seeking campaign, where those at risk of harm could approach a pharmacy and *request a Mask-19* to signal that they were experiencing gendered violence (Higgins, 2020). The pharmacy staff would then contact emergency services. A similar codeword strategy was launched in the UK at the beginning of 2021. The Ask for ANI (Action Needed Immediately) codeword scheme was developed by the UK Home Office in partnership with the domestic abuse sector, pharmacies and police (Home Office, 2022). Victim-survivors could visit participating pharmacies and use the codeword to discretely access support through pharmacy workers (Home Office, 2022).

Many DFV services providers established hidden services to enable covert communication with clients during lockdowns. These hidden services were invisible to other users and, most importantly, not captured in individuals' internet histories, which minimises the risk that abusers discover their online activities. In Australia, a common form of covert communication adopted by DFV service providers was the use of confidential mobile applications (Pfitzner et al., 2020a). One example of this is Gruveo, an encrypted web-based video call link that does not require users to download an app, making it undetectable on devices (Pfitzner et al., 2020a). During the lockdowns in Australia, there was also greater use of the Daisy app, which was available prior to the pandemic and developed by 1800RESPECT, a free national domestic, family and sexual violence counselling service. This free app provides information to users about local support services (1800RESPECT, n.d.). It includes several safety features aimed at protecting users' privacy. These include enabling users to add trusted contacts that do not have to be listed in the phone's contact list, visiting websites within the app so that sites do not appear in users' browser history, and 'quick exit' and 'get help' buttons (WESNET, 2020). In another example, the Italian government adapted the State Police app *YouPol*, which was initially developed to report teenage bullying, to receive domestic violence reports (Santagostino Recavarren & Elefante, 2020; Talmazan et al., 2020). Reports could be made by victim-survivors, family members and neighbours, and could be submitted anonymously through the app (Santagostino Recavarren & Elefante, 2020).

A similar covert communication strategy for providing access to DFV support using a digital platform was developed by Krystyna Paszko, a Polish high school student (Bretan, 2021; Easton, 2021). This student created a fake online cosmetic store called Camomiles and Pansies, where victim-survivors could receive online support from a psychologist (Bretan,

2021; Easton, 2021). When a victim-survivor asked to buy a particular cream, they would receive a response from a psychologist asking how long they had been suffering from the skin problem (Bretan, 2021; Easton, 2021). Victim-survivors could signal to authorities that they were at immediate risk of harm and required a home welfare check by placing an order and leaving their address (Bretan, 2021; Easton, 2021).

These examples demonstrate how concerns about client privacy and confidentiality together with reports of increased perpetrator surveillance of communication technology have prompted many agencies to explore ways of providing remote support without detection (Pfitzner et al., 2022b). Confidential mobile applications, codewords and covert signalling are all examples of interventions developed by services providers to overcome barriers related to the accommodation dimension of access. These innovative interventions were designed to allow individuals to alert support services and authorities to their situation, to report violence and to receive help without their abuser's knowledge.

Increasing the Accessibility of DFV Support Services During Lockdowns

In addition to providing alternative and covert pathways into DFV support during the lockdowns, many DFV services developed strategies to overcome barriers relating to geographic accessibility during periods of lockdown. In some countries, DFV services partnered with private sector organisations to provide secure transportation to shelters and safe housing for victim-survivors fleeing abusive relationships during lockdowns. For instance, France's National Federation of Solidarity for Women partnered with the ride-share company Uber to provide free rides for people feeling domestic violence during the pandemic (Campistron, 2020). Uber formed similar partnerships with civil society organisations across the world to provide free rides to shelters for people escaping domestic violence during the pandemic (Black, 2020; DC Coalition Against Domestic Violence, 2020).

In Australia, several DFV service providers partnered with the all-woman-run ride-share service Shebah and the goods delivery service SheDrops to provide access to services for clients. Agencies reported using Shebah to transport clients experiencing DFV to safe houses and alternative accommodation during lockdowns (Pfitzner et al., 2020a). SheDrops was also utilised to provide material aid to clients who were unable to travel to facilities to collect goods during periods of stay-at-home orders (Pfitzner et al., 2020a).

While private sector partnerships are not unique to the COVID-19 pandemic, housing insecurity is a, if not the, priority concern for victim-survivors escaping DFV (Flanagan et al., 2019; Love, 2021; Rollins et al., 2013). These public–private partnerships developed during the pandemic facilitated direct access to DFV services and safe housing for victim-survivors leaving abusive homes.

Acceptability: Perpetrators and Access to Support Services During COVID-19

The increased demand on DFV services internationally during the COVID-19 pandemic also applied to services that work with perpetrators of DFV. In Australia during the initial lockdown in early 2020, the average number of weekly referred calls to the Men's Referral Service, a national telephone counselling service operated by No to Violence (NTV), increased by more than 400 calls a week compared to the same period in 2019 (Tuohy, 2020). The widescale transition to phone, message, video and web-based service delivery models by victim support services also triggered exploration of remote delivery models for perpetrator interventions (Pfitzner et al., 2020b).

Acceptability is a central concern for services that work with perpetrators as the stigmatised nature of DFV services can hinder psychological accessibility (Pfitzner et al., 2017; Weeks, 2004). Psychological accessibility refers to individuals' perceptions of the service delivery environment acknowledging that social and cultural attitudes may inhibit or facilitate access to services. Keen to retain perpetrators already engaged in support services during the lockdowns, NTV—the Australian peak body for organisations working with men to end DFV—developed the Brief Intervention Service (BIS) (No to Violence [NTV], 2020). The BIS is a multi-session phone service for men perpetrating DFV and is funded by the Australian Government Department of Social Services (NTV, 2020). The phone service commenced operation in July 2020 during the nation's toughest lockdown conditions and was available to men who were unable to access DFV support during the lockdowns, who were on waiting lists for such support or who had concerns about their behaviour during the lockdowns (NTV, 2020). The provision of a multi-session remote, phone-based service for men using violence marked a distinct shift in practice principles in Australia. Prior to the COVID-19 pandemic, many people in the Australian men's service sector had reservations about the effectiveness of remote perpetrator interventions in terms of accountability, avoidance and partner safety (NTV & Men's Referral Services, 2015; Pfitzner et al., 2020b; Victorian State Government, 2018). Coinciding with the introduction of the BIS, the Victorian Government in partnership with NTV published *Service Guidelines for perpetrator interventions during the coronavirus (COVID-19) pandemic* (Family Safety Victoria, 2020). These guidelines set out a multi-intervention service model designed to support practitioners while they transitioned services to remote delivery during the restrictions and then back to in-person delivery afterwards. The model set out the type of intervention that can be provided by risk level, frequency, eligibility and outcome (Family Safety Victoria, 2020).

Much of the work on remote service responses to DFV during the COVID-19 pandemic has centred on enabling access to support for victim-survivors who were locked down with an abuser. The BIS example reminds us that greater practice innovation to promote access to support services by perpetrators is also required to ensure that abusers are kept in view and held to account.

Concluding Thoughts

During times of crisis and disaster ensuring access to, and continuity of, support for individuals affected by DFV is paramount. The interconnections between crises, disasters and increased DFV is well documented (Hozic & True, 2016; Kinnvall & Rydstrom, 2019). The COVID-19 pandemic has raised unique challenges for DFV services which have faced unprecedented demand and new barriers to service use. Internationally, DFV service providers have innovated and adapted their traditionally in-person, face-to-face interactions with clients. The COVID-19 pandemic has seen a large shift to providing support via phone, web, video and message-based services. Mindful of confidentiality and safety concerns during periods of stay-at-home orders, service providers have reimagined access channels and utilised covert communication to allow individuals to seek support without their abusers' knowledge.

The transition to remote service delivery models during the pandemic has not been without challenge. The effectiveness of remote risk assessments and safety planning remains in question (Cortis et al., 2021; Pfitzner et al., 2022b). The omnipresence of perpetrators in homes during lockdowns has adversely impacted the ability of victim-survivors to have full and frank discussions with service providers about safety concerns (Pfitzner et al., 2020a). Practitioners have lamented the loss of the visual cues provided through face-to-face work and reported that providing support remotely hinders their ability to build rapport and trust with clients (Cortis et al., 2021; Pfitzner et al., 2022a).

Overall, the existing research suggests that remote service delivery models increase access for some clients while inhibiting service use for others. The use of digital interventions by DFV service providers during the COVID-19 pandemic has given rise to a number of tensions. For instance, the tension between the demand for flexibility and the challenges encountered in building trust digitally with traumatised clients, particularly those with historically low levels of trust in public institutions (Battaglia et al., 2003; Messing et al., 2022; Richardson Foster et al., 2022). Previous research on the use of online supports by women experiencing domestic violence in health care systems indicates that online services are not only convenient but also offer users greater control over help-seeking processes (Tarzia et al., 2018). At the same time, digital interventions can impact on relationship and trust-building between users and service providers (Bracewell et al., 2020).

The pivot to remote service delivery also generated new tensions regarding equity in physical access to services. Remote service models provided greater equity of access for rural users and clients with mobility disabilities, but reduced access for digitally low-literate users and those without access to the internet (Richardson Foster et al., 2022; Tarzia et al., 2018). The COVID-19 pandemic has made the inequity between socio-economic households and access to care systems unmistakably clear. During the pandemic, the digital divide had given rise to new forms of disadvantage with victim-survivors who lack access to high-speed internet and WiFi-enabled devices and/or with low levels of digital literacy having limited or no access to support.

An unignorable gap in the service innovation evidence base is the general absence of research into the user experience (for a notable exception, see Richardson Foster et al., 2022). To date, little information has been collected from victim-survivors about their experiences of receiving support remotely during the pandemic, particularly what mode(s) of interaction worked for which clients and in what circumstances. The service adaptions and innovations identified in this chapter largely come from studies with practitioners and service providers. Further research is needed to better understand the lived help-seeking experiences of victim-survivors throughout the pandemic to inform improved services responses in future crises and learnings that can be incorporated into services models in the 'new normal'.

Bibliography

1800RESPECT. (n.d.). *Daisy app.* https://www.1800respect.org.au/daisy

Agence France-Presse in Geneva. (2021, December 1). More than a third of world's population have never used internet, says UN. *The Guardian.* https://www.theguardian.com/technology/2021/nov/30/more-than-a-third-of-worlds-population-has-never-used-the-internet-says-un

Bagheri Lankarani, K., Hemyari, C., Honarvar, B., et al. (2022). Domestic violence and associated factors during COVID-19 epidemic: An online population-based study in Iran. *BMC Public Health, 22*(1), 774. https://doi.org/10.1186/s12889-022-12536-y

Battaglia, T. A., Finley, E., & Liebschutz, J. M. (2003). Survivors of intimate partner violence speak out: Trust in the patient-provider relationship. *Journal of General Internal Medicine, 18*(8), 617–623. https://doi.org/10.1046/j.1525-1497.2003.21013.x

Black, M. (2020, April 30). Uber offers free rides for people fleeing domestic violence during COVID-19 pandemic. *Global Citizen.* https://www.globalcitizen.org/en/content/uber-offers-free-rides-for-people-fleeing-domestic/

Bracewell, K., Hargreaves, P., & Stanley, N. (2020). The consequences of the Covid-19 lockdown on stalking victimisation. *Journal of Family Violence, 37*(6), 951–957. https://doi.org/10.1007/s10896-020-00201-0

Bretan, J. (2021, July 19). How one high schooler's Facebook beauty brand is saving survivors of domestic abuse in Poland. *The Calvert Journal.* https://www.calvertjournal.com/features/show/12909/facebook-beauty-brand-domestic-abuse-poland

Boxall, H., Morgan, A., & Brown, R. (2020). *The prevalence of domestic violence among women during the COVID-19 pandemic* (Statistical Bulletin No 28). Australian Institute of Criminology. https://www.aic.gov.au/publications/sb/sb28

Campistron, M. (2020, November 2). France fears fresh wave of domestic violence amid second Covid-19 lockdown. *France24*. https://www.france24. com/en/france/20201102-france-fears-fresh-wave-of-domestic-violence-amid-second-covid-19-lockdown

Cortis, N., Smyth, C., Valentine, K., Breckenridge, J., & Cullen, P. (2021). Adapting service delivery during COVID-19: Experiences of domestic violence practitioners. *British Journal of Social Work, 51*(5), 1779–1798. https://doi.org/10.1093/bjsw/bcab105

DC Coalition Against Domestic Violence (DCCADV). (2020, April 22). *Uber initiative includes 1,000 free rides for survivors and advocates.* https://dccadv.org/2020/04/uber-initiative-includes-1000-free-rides-for-survivors-and-advocates/

Easton, A. (2021, March 1). Why this teen set up a prize-winning fake cosmetics shop. *BBC News*. https://www.bbc.com/news/world-europe-56172456

Family Safety Victoria. (2020). *Service guidelines for perpetrator interventions during the coronavirus (COVID-19) pandemic.* https://fac.dhhs.vic.gov. au/news/releasedservice-guidelines-perpetrator-interventions-during-corona virus-covid-19-pandemic

Flanagan, K., Blunden, H. V., Valentine, K., & Henriette, J. (2019). *Housing outcomes after domestic and family violence* (AHURI Final Report 311). http://www.ahuri.edu.au/research/final-reports/311

Higgins, N. (2020, April 13). Coronavirus: When home gets violent under lockdown in Europe, *BBC News*. https://www.bbc.com/news/world-europe-522 16966

Home Office (United Kingdom), & The Rt Hon Priti Patel MP. (2020, April 11). *Home Secretary announces support for domestic abuse victims.* https://www.gov.uk/government/news/home-secretary-announces-support-for-domestic-abuse-victims

Home Office (United Kingdom). (2022, May 12). *Ask for ANI domestic abuse codeword: Information for pharmacies.* https://www.gov.uk/guidance/ask-for-ani-domestic-abuse-codeword-information-for-pharmacies

Hozic, A. A., & True, J. (2016). *Scandalous economics: Gender and the politics of financial crises*. Oxford University Press.

Inter-Agency Standing Committee (IASC) & Global Protection Cluster: GBV Prevention and Response (GPC). (2020). *Identifying & mitigating gender-based violence risks within the COVID-19 response.* https://gbvguidelines. org/wp/wp-content/uploads/2020/04/Interagency-GBV-risk-mitigation-and-Covid-tipsheet.pdf

International Planned Parenthood Federation. (2020, April 22). *COVID-19 and the rise of gender-based violence.* https://www.ippf.org/blogs/covid-19-and-rise-gender-based-violence

Joshi, A., Paterson, N., Hinkley, T., & Joss, N. (2021). *The use of telepractice in the family and relationship services sector* (CFCA Paper 57). Australian Institute of Family Studies. https://aifs.gov.au/sites/default/files/public ation-documents/2104_cfca_57_the_use_of_telepractice_in_the_family_and_ relationship_services_sector_0.pdf

Kinnvall, C., & Rydstrom, H. (Eds.). (2019). *Climate hazards, disasters, and gender ramifications. Routledge series in hazards, disaster risk and climate change.* Routledge.

Lauve-Moon, K., & Ferreira, R. J. (2020). An exploratory investigation: Post-disaster predictors of intimate partner violence. *Clinical Social Work Journal, 45,* 124–135. http://doi.org/10.1007/s10615-015-0572-z

Lee, J., Flint, J., & McIntosh, J. (2017, December 1). *E-screening to connect the dots on risks to family wellbeing: A literature review.* Paper presented at the Family & Relationship Services Australia National Conference. http://frsa. org.au/wp-content/uploads/2018/01/FFRSA-conference-ejournal-4.pdf

Lock, H. (2020, April 11). Priti Patel announces new campaign to tackle rise in domestic abuse during coronavirus lockdown. *iNews.* https://inews.co. uk/news/priti-patel-announces-campaign-rise-domestic-abuse-during-corona virus-lockdown-417784

Love, C. (2021, December 20). Housing instability a top concern for survivors of domestic violence, a new report says. *Houston Public Media.* https:// www.houstonpublicmedia.org/articles/news/health-science/2021/12/20/ 415825/housing-instability-top-concern-for-survivors-of-domestic-violence/

Martin, J., McBride, T., Masterman, T., Pote, I., Mokhtar, N., Oprea, E., & Sorgenfrei, M. (2020). *Covid-19 and early intervention evidence, challenges and risks relating to virtual and digital delivery.* Early Intervention Foundation. https://www.eif.org.uk/report/covid-19-and-early-int ervention-evidence-challenges-and-risks-relating-to-virtual-and-digital-delivery

McLaughlin, C. G., & Wyszewianski, L. (2002). Access to care: Remembering old lessons. *Health Services Research, 37*(6), 1441–1443. https://doi.org/10. 1111/1475-6773.12171

Messing, J., Wachter, K., AbiNader, M., Ward-Lasher, A., Njie-Carr, V., Sabri, B., Murray, S., Noor-Oshiro, A., & Campbell, J. (2022). "We Have to Build Trust": Intimate partner violence risk assessment with immigrant and refugee survivors. *Social Work Research, 46*(1), 53–64. https://doi.org/10.1093/ swr/svab030

No to Violence (NTV). (2020, July 13). *Key changes to the MRS.* https://ntv. org.au/key-changes-to-the-mrs/

No to Violence, & Men's Referral Services. (2015). *Strengthening perpetrator accountability within the Victorian family violence service system.* http:// rcfv.archive.royalcommission.vic.gov.au/getattachment/E771CDC5-4D7C-4638-B3EE-546EA32871F1/Men-s-Referral-Service;-No-To-Violence.pdf

O'Donnell, O. (2007). Access to health care in developing countries: Breaking down demand side barriers. *Cadernos De Saúde Pública, 23*(12), 2820–2834. https://doi.org/10.1590/s0102-311x2007001200003

Onyango, M. A., & Regan, A. (2020, 10 May). Sexual and gender-based violence during COVID-19: Lessons from Ebola. *The Conversation.* Retrieved from https://theconversation.com/sexual-and-gender-based-violence-during-covid-19-lessons-from-ebola-137541

Owen, L. (2020, March 8). Coronavirus: Five ways virus upheaval is hitting women in Asia. *BBC News.* https://www.bbc.com/news/world-asia-517 05199

Parkinson, D., & Zara, C. (2013). The hidden disaster: Domestic violence in the aftermath of natural disaster. *The Australian Journal of Emergency Management, 28*(2), 28–35.

Penchansky, R., & Thomas, J. W. (1981). The concept of access: Definition and relationship to consumer satisfaction. *Medical Care, 19*(2), 127–140.

Peterman, A., Potts, A., O'Donnell, M., Thompson, K., Shah, N., Oertelt-Prigione, S., & van Gelder, N. (2020). *Pandemics and Violence Against Women and Children* (CGD Working Paper 528). Center for Global Development. https://www.cgdev.org/publication/pandemics-and-violence-against-women-and-children

Peters, D. H., Garg, A., Bloom, G., Walker, D. G., Brieger, W. R., & Hafizur Rahman, M. (2008). Poverty and access to health care in developing countries. *Annals of the New York Academy of Sciences, 1136*(1), 161–171. https://doi.org/10.1196/annals.1425.011

Pfitzner, N., Fitz-Gibbon, K., & True, J. (2020a). *Responding to the 'shadow pandemic': Practitioner views on the nature of and responses to violence against women in Victoria, Australia during the COVID-19 restrictions.* Monash University. https://doi.org/10.26180/5ed9d5198497c

Pfitzner, N., Fitz-Gibbon, K., McGowan, J., & True, J. (2020b). *When home becomes the workplace: Family violence, practitioner wellbeing and remote service delivery during COVID-19 restrictions.* Monash University. https://doi.org/10.26180/13108352

Pfitzner, N., Fitz-Gibbon, K., & Meyer, S. (2022a). Responding to women experiencing domestic and family violence during the COVID-19 pandemic: Exploring experiences and impacts of remote service delivery in Australia. *Child & Family Social Work, 27*(1), 30–40. https://doi.org/10.1111/cfs.12870

Pfitzner, N., Fitz-Gibbon, K., & True, J. (2022b). When staying home isn't safe: Australian practitioner experiences of responding to intimate partner violence during COVID-19 restrictions. *Journal of Gender-Based Violence,* 1–18. https://doi.org/10.1332/239868021X16420024310873

Pfitzner, N., Humphreys, C., & Hegarty, K. (2017). Research review: Engaging men: A multi-level model to support father engagement. *Child & Family Social Work, 22*(1), 537–547. https://doi.org/10.1111/cfs.1225

Piquero, A. R., Wesley, G. J., Jemison, E., Kaukinen, C., & Knaul, F. M. (2021). Domestic violence during COVID-19: Evidence from a systematic review and meta-analysis. *Journal of Criminal Justice, 74*, 101806. https://doi.org/10.1016/j.jcrimjus.2021.101806

Pugh, A., Castleden, H., Giesbrecht, M., Davison, C., & Crooks, V. (2019). Awareness as a dimension of health care access. *Journal of Health Services Research & Policy, 24*(2), 108–115. https://doi.org/10.1177/1355819619829782

Richardson Foster, H., Bracewell, K., Farrelly, N., Barter, C., Chantler, K., Howarth, E., & Stanley, N. (2022). Experience of specialist DVA provision under COVID-19: Listening to service user voices to shape future practice. *Journal of Gender-Based Violence, 6*(3), 409–425. https://doi.org/10.1332/239868021X16442400262389

Rollins, C., Billhardt, K., & Olsen, L. (2013). *Housing: Safety, stability, and signity for survivors of domestic violence*. https://wscadv.org/wp-content/uploads/2015/05/DVHF_SafetyPaper2013-final.pdf

Santagostino Recavarren, I., & Elefante, M. (2020, October 1). *The shadow pandemic: Violence against women during COVID-19*. World Bank Blogs. https://blogs.worldbank.org/developmenttalk/shadow-pandemic-violence-against-women-during-covid-19

Saurman, E. (2016). Improving access. *Journal of Health Services Research & Policy, 21*(1), 36–39. https://doi.org/10.1177/1355819615600001

Talmazan, Y., Sirna,L., Muñoz Ratto, H., & Ing, N. (2020, April 3). European countries develop new ways to tackle domestic violence during coronavirus lockdowns. *NBC News*. https://www.nbcnews.com/news/world/european-countries-develop-new-ways-tackle-domestic-violence-during-coronavirus-n1174301

Tarzia, L., Cornelio, R., Forsdike, K., & Hegarty, K. (2018). Women's experiences receiving support online for intimate partner violence: How does it compare to face-to-face support from a health professional? *Interacting with Computers, 30*(5), 433–443. https://doi.org/10.1093/iwc/iwy019

True, J. (2013). Gendered violence in natural disasters: Learning from New Orleans, Haiti and Christchurch. *Aotearoa New Zealand Social Work, 25*(2), 78–89.

Tuohy, W. (2020, April 12). Helpline calls by family violence perpetrators 'skyrocket' amid isolation. *The Age*. https://www.theage.com.au/national/victoria/helpline-calls-by-family-violence-perpetrators-skyrocket-amid-isolation-20200410-p54iw7.html

United Nations Interregional Crime and Justice Research Institute (UNICRI). (2015). *The impacts of the crisis on gender equality and women's wellbeing in EU Mediterranean countries.* http://www.unicri.it/news/files/VAW_draft_last_lowq.pdf

Victorian State Government. (2018). *Expert Advisory Committee on Perpetrator Interventions* (Final Report). https://www.vic.gov.au/sites/default/files/2019-10/Expert-Advisory-Committee-on-Perpetrator-Interventions-Final-Report-Accessibility-Version_0.docx

Weeks, W. (2004). Creating attractive services which citizens want to attend. *Australian Social Work, 57*(4), 319–330.

WESNET. (2020). *Daisy App.* https://techsafety.org.au/resources/appsafetycentre/apps-reviewed/daisy-app/

CHAPTER 6

Helping from Home: DFV Worker Wellbeing During the 'Shadow Pandemic'

Abstract Historically, there has been limited attention paid to the support needs of the domestic and family violence workforce beyond a general emphasis on self-care in social work training. Drawing on an Australian case study, this chapter examines why the COVID-19 pandemic has sharply highlighted the need to pay attention to the wellbeing of those specialist practitioners working remotely to support women experiencing DFV during stay-at-home restrictions.

Keywords Practitioner wellbeing · Trauma work · Care work · Domestic and family violence workforce · COVID-19

INTRODUCTION

The first two years of the COVID-19 pandemic shone a spotlight on care work of all kinds. While there has been increasing recognition of the emotional toll of care work during the pandemic, to date support has been limited to specific types of care workers. The mental health and wellbeing of health care workers have been a priority consideration in government responses internationally to COVID-19 (Blake et al., 2021; Department of Health, 2020; Dow, 2020; Kinman et al., 2020; Sainato, 2020; Yaker, 2020). This focus on health care worker wellbeing was

© The Author(s) 2023

N. Pfitzner et al., *Violence Against Women During Coronavirus*,
https://doi.org/10.1007/978-3-031-29356-6_6

informed by previous research that demonstrated the negative psychological effects of health crises on health care workers including anxiety, stress, depression, burnout and post-traumatic stress disorder (Cabarkapa et al., 2020; Preti et al., 2020; Sanghera et al., 2020; Stuijfzand et al., 2020). Notably, there has not been the same level of government mobilisation to safeguard the mental health and wellbeing of DFV workers on the frontline of the so-called 'shadow pandemic' of violence against women. The COVID-19 pandemic has placed extraordinary demands on DFV service systems worldwide. Like their health and aged care colleagues, DFV workers have experienced unprecedented demand since the onset of the pandemic (Boserup et al., 2020; Campbell, 2020; Carrington et al., 2021; Pfitzner et al., 2020a, 2020b, 2022a, 2022b). With people sheltering in homes during government-directed lockdowns, DFV has intensified in both prevalence and severity (Bagheri Lankarani et al., 2022; Boxall et al., 2020; Pfitzner et al., 2020a, 2022b; Piquero et al., 2021).

The onset of the pandemic triggered the closure of workplaces, schools and childcare facilities and a global transition to working from home. For most DFV workers, this meant that home became the primary setting for performing their professional paid care work, and often unpaid childcare and schooling. This chapter explores how the COVID-19 pandemic and the shift to working from home impacted the mental health and emotional wellbeing of DFV specialist workers.

Working with Domestic and Family Violence Clients

Working with traumatised clients, such as individuals and families who have experienced or are experiencing DFV, often unavoidably affects professional and personal functioning (Cohen & Collens, 2013; McCann & Pearlman, 1990). Secondary traumatic stress (STS), vicarious trauma (VT), compassion fatigue, burnout and occupational stress have been identified as common responses to the challenging nature of trauma work (Brend et al., 2020; Choi, 2011; Cohen & Collens, 2013; Kulkarni et al., 2013; McCann & Pearlman, 1990; Morran, 2008; Tarshis & Baird, 2019). Figley (1995, p. 7) defines STS as, 'the natural consequent behaviours and emotions resulting from knowing about a traumatizing event experienced by a significant other—the stress resulting from helping or wanting to help a traumatized or suffering person'. In contrast, VT refers to the process in which professionals working with trauma survivors can become negatively affected by their clients' traumatic experiences (McCann & Pearlman, 1990). Hearing clients' stories of trauma can alter professionals' sense of self and how they see the world. They can become more fearful or cynical, unable to trust and develop connections with others, experience depression and develop feelings of powerlessness (McCann & Pearlman, 1990). While there is some debate about how these constructs are conceptualised (see Brend et al., 2020), as suggested in what follows, there is an evidence-based consensus that working with people impacted by trauma has negative effects on worker wellbeing.

These negative effects on wellbeing extend beyond individual practitioners and have wider implications for the DFV workforce in terms of high staff turnover and low employee retention. For example, a 2017 DFV workforce census in Victoria, Australia, revealed that almost one-third of specialist DFV practitioners were considering leaving their job due to burnout (Family Safety Victoria, 2017). COVID-19 has presented unique challenges for DFV sectors internationally. Public health orders have required DFV services to adapt and innovate in response to constantly changing work conditions while services simultaneously experienced increased demand. The following discussion explores the mental health and wellbeing implications of working during the COVID-19 pandemic for DFV workforces through a case study examination of the experiences of practitioners in Victoria.

TRAUMA CARE DURING THE COVID-19 CRISIS: AN AUSTRALIAN CASE STUDY

As in many countries around the world, Australian states and territories entered government-directed lockdowns in March 2020, which involved orders to work from home and significant restrictions on movement intended to curb the spread of COVID-19.[1] In the Australian state of Victoria, a state of emergency was declared on 16 March 2020. By the end of March, the state entered its first lockdown (also referred to as

---

[1] In Australia, COVID-19 lockdowns and restrictions were state and territory-based. All state and territories enacted restrictions in March 2020 (see Storen & Corrigan, 2020).

Stage 3 restrictions), where people could only go outside their home for four permitted reasons: shopping for food and necessary goods, providing care, exercising and work or education that individuals were unable to do either from home.

An online survey of 166 Victorian DFV practitioners conducted by Pfitzner et al. (2020a, 2022b) in 2020 investigated the impact of COVID-19 and associated restrictions on women's experiences of DFV in Victoria.[2] The survey revealed that practitioners perceived that the prevalence, severity and nature of DFV experienced by their clients had intensified during the first 2020 lockdown. The DFV practitioners reported that their clients' experiences of DFV had increased in frequency by 59% and increased in severity by 50% during the initial lockdown (Pfitzner et al., 2020a, 2022b). The survey findings aligned with data later released by Victoria Police which showed that the number of police-recorded DFV incidents was higher every month in 2020 compared to 2019 (Rmandic et al., 2020).

In addition to collecting data on DFV trends observed among specialist DFV practitioners, the survey captured the impact of COVID-19 and the associated lockdowns on DFV services. In Victoria, the DFV workforce were not classified as essential workers exempt from the work-from-home orders and DFV workers had to rapidly transition to supporting people affected by violence remotely from their homes. Prior to the COVID-19 pandemic, Victorian DFV services, like their interstate and international counterparts, were based on in-person face-to-face service delivery models (Joshi et al., 2021; Lee et al., 2017; Martin et al., 2020). When asked about the impact of the pandemic on their service delivery, a few practitioners flagged concerns about increased stress and the greater potential for vicarious trauma during the lockdowns:

---

[2] The online survey of practitioners responding to DFV ran for a four-week period from 23 April to 24 May 2020 during Victoria's first lockdown. The anonymous online survey combined a series of short demographic questions with rating scale and open-ended questions. Respondents could choose to answer some or all of the survey questions, which invited practitioners to reflect on the impact of COVID-19 restrictions on women's experiences of IPV and their own experience of providing support during lockdown, including practice changes and service adaptations. Questions about the perceptions of the impact of the pandemic on the prevalence and nature of violence were measured using scale variables where 1–2 represented a decrease, 3 no change and 4–5 an increase.

Increased stress on clinicians due to the pressure to not place the client at greater risk of harm when delivering an adapted service model whilst the client is in isolation with the perpetrator. (DFV practitioner, survey one respondent)

Difficulties supporting staff and assisting with vicarious trauma and holding risk in relation to women and children. (DFV practitioner, survey one respondent)

The first lockdown in Victoria lasted around six weeks and restrictions began to ease from mid-May through to 1 June 2020. In late June 2020, restrictions began to tighten again and the Melbourne metropolitan area and the Mitchell Shire re-entered Stage 3 restrictions on 9 July. Under Stage 3, people were required to stay at home and could only go outside for the four permitted reasons previously listed. On 23 July, two weeks after returning to Stage 3 restrictions, the wearing of face coverings outside the home was made compulsory in these two areas of Victoria. Following the continued increase in daily coronavirus infection numbers, a state of disaster was declared in Victoria on 2 August and some of the world's most stringent restrictions came into place. The entire Melbourne metropolitan area entered Stage 4, which included the additional imposition of a nightly curfew from 8 p.m. to 5 a.m., limiting people's movements to a five kilometre radius from their homes unless they had an exemption, closing all kindergarten and day care centres except for children of permitted workers, restricting household shopping to one person per household per day, and limiting daily outdoor exercise to one hour per person. These restrictions lasted until 28 October 2020 when government orders shifted from 'stay-at-home' to 'stay safe', and the four permitted reasons to leave home no longer applied.

During the height of the Stage 4 restrictions in Victoria, Pfitzner et al. (2020b) conducted a second state-wide study that investigated the impact of the prolonged lockdown on DFV worker wellbeing. The study was based on an online survey of 113 Victorian DFV practitioners[3] and virtual

---

[3] The online survey ran for a four-week period from 13 July to 9 August 2020. It combined a series of short demographic questions with a rating scale and open-ended questions. The questions invited practitioners to reflect on the personal benefits and challenges of working remotely, the supports needed to safeguard their wellbeing during the pandemic as well as service innovations that have emerged during this time, and the infrastructure required to support these practice changes over the long term. As part of the

focus groups with 28 practitioners from specialist DFV and men's services conducted during July–August 2020.[4] The study findings revealed that working from home and providing DFV support remotely exacerbated the psychological impact of caring for trauma survivors. In particular, the loss of in-person, on-site collegial support and debriefing, and the erosion of personal boundaries due to working from home had significant adverse effects on worker wellbeing. These research findings are explored in the following discussion under three themes: the cost of care work during a crisis, when home becomes the workplace, and the loss of in-person peer support and debriefing.

The Cost of Care Work During a Crisis

A major theme arising from the second Victoria study, which looked at the impact of lockdowns on DFV worker wellbeing, was the challenges of working during a time of crisis. Many of the focus group participants reported that the constant uncertainty of the COVID-19 pandemic was negatively affecting their work and mental health. As one practitioner noted:

> I've literally got to get online on our intranet and check the working instructions practically every day or when there's a situation come up because they change so rapidly. It's just so hard to keep on top of all the changes. (Specialist DFV practitioner, focus group participant)

Similar sentiments were made by one survey participant in response to a question about personal challenges associated with working during the pandemic. In nominating challenges associated with working during the pandemic, the survey respondent said that they were 'constantly needing to review process and procedure to ensure safety'.

DFV workers not only experienced an unprecedent increased in the volume and intensity of their work but they also had to rapidly adapt

---

focus on worker wellbeing, respondents were asked to complete the Professional Quality of Life Scale Version 5 (ProQOL).

[4] The online focus groups were conducted in the four-week period immediately following the survey closure in August 2020. The focus groups and interviews were semi-structured with respondents answering open-ended questions on worker wellbeing and service innovations.

their services and programs to provide support remotely and faced ever changing pandemic-mandated protocols. As one practitioner explained:

> So as the different lockdowns have happened, different stages, different requirements in terms of whether it's PPE or contingency plans. Like having to constantly revise things and update things and then communicate what that means now. That's generated a lot of work and demand too … So even just trying to keep on top of all of that as well has been quite challenging whilst we're still trying to run the program and support staff and manage any crises or whatever else. It's just been really complicated and complex. (Specialist DFV practitioner, focus group participant)

The inability of workers to provide in-person support due to COVID-19 restrictions along with the uncertainty of what was occurring in homes affected by DFV during this time, compounded the general stress and anxiety felt by the DFV workforce. As one worker said:

> Whereas previously we might have employed a strategy of just dropping by to visit a client, now I think if a client's not engaging there's that real concern about what's happening for them and how long it's been since a worker has actually sighted them to know how they actually are, and if they're ok. I think definitely workers are carrying that weight and I think yeah, I'm really conscious of the impact of that on workers as well, having to sit with that uncertainty and try and find ways of sort of doing what we can to manage risk. (Specialist DFV practitioner, focus group participant)

With the DFV service system overwhelmed due to high demand during the second state lockdown, workers felt an increased emotional burden caring for clients:

> There's a lot of hoops to go through to get from A to B all of a sudden because of all the restrictions in place … I actually described it yesterday that it felt like someone had just poured a heap of concrete on my shoulders because my client had put so much trust and – just all onto me, and I literally felt that weight and it was like okay, it's up to me to do this for her now. (Specialist DFV practitioner, focus group participant)

Providing professional care to people impacted by trauma, such as DFV, can be stressful during non-catastrophic conditions. In Victoria, the lockdowns and associated restrictions necessitated a rapid transition to remote service delivery models, which limited DFV service responses and slowed system processes. These restricted working conditions escalated the stress and emotional burden experienced by workers who provide support to individuals affected by DFV. In addition to heightening the psychological consequences of working with clients experiencing trauma, the COVID-19 pandemic also saw the home become the workplace for most DFV professionals.

When Home Becomes the Workplace

Working from home and the associated COVID-19 restrictions undid traditional self-care strategies employed by DFV workers. A key feature of effective self-care strategies for DFV workers is separating work and personal life often through creating a safe space that is physically and psychologically removed from the workplace. The majority of the DFV workers in this second Victorian study reported that their safe space was typically their home. Prior to the COVID-19 pandemic, most DFV services in Victoria were delivered through face-to-face interactions with clients that took place at on-site facilities or during client home visits. These on-site working models meant that DFV practitioners did not conduct work from home.

The second Victorian study showed that the transition to working from home during the pandemic allowed clients' trauma stories to infiltrate workers' homes and erode their self-care practices. As practitioners reflected:

> Challenging to bring family violence trauma into my home "my safe space". Challenging to maintain work/home divide. (DFV practitioner, survey two respondent)

> It just feels like there's this hum of family violence in this room and it's become this – when it's all over I feel like I need to sage the room and do all this stuff. (Specialist DFV practitioner, focus group participant)

> I currently work out of my bedroom. This makes it difficult to uphold work/life boundaries. It's not ideal talking about highly emotional / traumatic / violent things in my own bedroom. It taints the feeling of my bedroom being a safe space and it's more difficult to switch off after work. (DFV practitioner, survey two respondent)

Workers also said they had difficulty 'switching off' when working from home. As part of their mental health and wellbeing strategies prior to the pandemic, some workers engaged in end-of-workday rituals to create a separation from work and tune out from their day. This often happened on their commute home or in carparks at workplaces. However, practitioners said that working from home did not provide the same opportunities to symbolically and mentally mark the end of their working day, and it was difficult to separate their work and personal lives:

> There's just not that transition time between home and work ... I've heard colleagues talk about they can't walk into the car together. [It] felt like a really important part of the day ... When you just have a two-second walk from your spare bedroom to the kitchen, and the kids are there ready to be parented, it's very different. There's not a lot of transition space between the two. (Specialist DFV worker, focus group participant)

> I had an hour and a half drive generally to and an hour and a half from work, so that was head time. So the biggest impact I had was I think not having any unwind time. Straight away you finish work and you're at home, that can be really difficult to manage. (Men's services worker, focus group participant)

The practitioners' reflections indicate that it has been challenging to replicate end-of-workday rituals when working remotely from home and that many traditional self-care strategies, particularly maintaining personal and professional boundaries, have not been possible during the pandemic. In the context of DFV, end-of-workday rituals assist workers in creating physical and psychological space from their trauma work, helping them leave their work at work. These findings suggest that working from home inhibits workers' efforts to manage the psychological effects of their trauma work.

THE LOSS OF IN-PERSON PEER SUPPORT AND DEBRIEFING

Peer support and debriefing with colleagues is a common self-care strategy employed by professionals working with people impacted by trauma to promote their mental health and wellbeing (Killian, 2008; Lee & Millier, 2013). This current study showed that working remotely from home during lockdowns physically isolated practitioners from their colleagues and led to an immediate loss of in-person peer support and debriefing with colleagues. As these practitioners commented:

> So if it's a difficult situation you can turn around and debrief with someone or go for a walk with a colleague, step out for a coffee, and suddenly without all of that it felt strange. (Specialist DFV practitioner, focus group participant)

> It's challenging to not have a team around you and colleagues to debrief with immediately after a difficult phone call. (DFV practitioner, survey two respondent)

Many practitioners reported feeling isolated when working from home:

> Feeling quite isolated and alone in the work. It's challenging staying in contact with other practitioners and organisations. (DFV practitioner, survey respondent)

> Less contact between colleagues ... feel socially disconnected from your team. Don't have the ability to debrief so end up sharing with my partner which isn't ideal. (DFV practitioner, survey two respondent)

Practitioners reported that this isolation was felt acutely by workers living alone during the work-from-home orders:

> In relation to vicarious trauma, it adds another layer being in the home ... So yeah, that's certainly adding on another layer in terms of there's no escape in a way, that we are in a home and especially for those who live on their own and can't have contact back with family and friends. (Specialist DFV practitioner, focus group participant)

> For staff that are on their own, having to contend with that isolation ... it's really, I can really see the difference for those staff members that are on their own, and just sort of speaking with them about making sure that they're connected and with other supports as well. (Specialist DFV practitioner, focus group participant)

Some agencies offered virtual debriefing sessions and remote supervision to staff. However, many practitioners and managers said that these remote wellbeing supports felt formalised and uncomfortable:

I guess not being able to have those quick debrief conversations with staff anymore. Like when you're in the office and you had a difficult phone call or they had a difficult phone call they could simply turn around or come and grab you and say "can we have a chat?" Now it's more of a formal process where they have to pick up the phone and call and if they get you, they get you. If not, it becomes more challenging. (Specialist DFV practitioner, focus group participant)

The group video debriefs, I'm not a huge fan to be honest. I just prefer the casual, the kind of ad hoc one-on-one spontaneous debriefs and that doesn't happen and I'm not just going to call someone. It just feels a bit contrived or weird or maybe they're busy. It's just not the same as seeing that someone's sitting at their desk and has a free moment for a chat. (Specialist DFV practitioner, focus group participant)

Many DFV workers lamented the loss of incidental support. Further adding to the discomfort associated with pre-scheduled remote debriefings, practitioners who participated in the focus groups said that working remotely burdened individual staff with the responsibility to proactively seek support. As one practitioner commented:

I do think it's hard as well because it's almost like we have to be the ones that are proactively reaching out if we're struggling, and if you're not really in the right headspace in order to pick up the phone and call someone, it can be really, really hard. Yeah, it's not like when you are in the office and are able just to swing around your chair and talk to someone, you know? It's actually like you can feel quite isolated … I wish there was less of this expectation … that it's on the worker to make contact if you're struggling. (Specialist DFV practitioner, focus group participant)

DFV workers explained that during this time of increased demand and high workloads, they were reluctant to formally seek out colleagues for support who may themselves be struggling. As one practitioner explained:

That burden, it feels like you're holding that risk all the time … We have a lot of informal catchups to debrief and talk, and we still do regular supervision and all of those things but it's very hard to actually pick up the phone and say, "I just had a really rough conversation" because you don't know what they're doing. You don't know if they're busy, they could be having a rough day, because we don't have that luxury of being able to look over the pod and say they're free … So, I know the support's there but I don't necessarily say, "Hey, I'm not doing great, can I have a debrief?" (Specialist DFV practitioner, focus group participant)

Likewise, one manager explained that:

> I think definitely that is something that's been missing in the moment. Like when you've had a difficult call at home and I think I've certainly just tried to really encourage people to, that it is OK to just call on a colleague or to call me, just to kind of debrief in the moment about that challenging call but I think because there's that additional step of having to pick up the phone rather than when we were working in the office, a colleague would actually just notice if someone had had a difficult call and would reach out to them. But I think now that the onus is on that person that's had that call. I think often people are not taking that step of making the call. (Specialist DFV practitioner, focus group participant)

At the same time that working from home reduced opportunities for professional peer support and debriefing, it brought another layer of people directly into contact with trauma. Practitioners reported that conducting trauma work from home had a negative impact on the well-being of individuals sharing homes with them during the restrictions. Many practitioners were concerned about the exposure of their children to traumatic stories during periods of work-from-home orders. As two practitioners commented:

> I try to make sure that they [my children] don't hear any of it but they see me working and they can obviously see my presentation … it's … something that I've always tried to keep away from my children and they are now seeing the stress and … they probably hear certain things as they walk past … and I feel like they've been a little exposed to it … So when they see me stressed, they know that someone might be in danger, so they just get stressed as well. (Specialist DFV practitioner, focus group participant)

> It came up because my daughter … said, "Oh mum, can I ask you something?" … I thought she was in her bedroom … it was really horrible … [I] … had to sit there and debrief with her. And she only heard a snippet of a conversation. (Specialist DFV practitioner, focus group participant)

Another practitioner talked about trying to plan her client consultations around her child's movements so as to minimise their exposure to trauma stories. They said:

> Some of the conversations that we have ... it's horrific stuff. And I know my daughter is 19 but she doesn't need to hear what some of the stuff that comes through ... I try and plan my day around it. So that I'm not having those particular specific conversations ... on those days at home. (Specialist DFV practitioner, focus group participant)

As discussed earlier in this chapter, separating work and personal life was seen to be a critical self-care strategy and this was undone by bringing trauma work into homes. Where DFV workers shared homes with others in the field, the ability to tune out and create distance from their work was particularly challenging. As one practitioner explained:

> I live in a two-bedroom apartment with two other people as well who also work in family violence and I think there has been an assumption about if you're a professional working from home that you do have a space where you can separate and keep the door closed and everything like that but that's not the reality ... And the vicarious trauma can be really impactful. I noticed within my housemates that their mental health significantly declined just from having a house that was just full of family violence talk. (Specialist DFV practitioner, focus group participant)

The empirical findings presented in this chapter clearly demonstrate the adverse outcomes on DFV professionals' mental health and wellbeing when trauma work is brought into their private spheres. The remote work settings during the COVID-19 pandemic fostered a sense of social isolation and loneliness among workers and reduced the availability and accessibility of peer support and debriefing. The loss of immediate, in-person peer support and debriefing with colleagues intensified the already significant psychological consequences for DFV professionals of exposure to their clients' traumatic experiences. In addition, this study shows that the negative psychological effects of providing trauma care from homes extended beyond workers directly providing care to other individuals sharing homes with them during periods of restrictions.

A Gendered Burden of Care: DFV
Workers and Unpaid Care Work
During the COVID-19 Pandemic

The gender asymmetries in unpaid care work are well documented, and so too is the mental health burden of such unpaid work (Ervin et al., 2022; Seedat & Rondon, 2021). Women have been awarded the unenviable label of the 'shock absorbers' of the COVID-19 pandemic and described as performing a 'double double shift' during lockdowns (John et al., 2020; Sandberg & Thomas, 2020). Prior to the pandemic, women and girls provided 75% of unpaid care and domestic work performed in homes each day worldwide (Moreira da Silva, 2019). The International Labour Organisation (2018) calculates that on average women spend 3.2 times more time on unpaid care work than men performing four hours and 25 minutes of unpaid care work each day compared to only one hour and 23 minutes for men. These gendered differences in the proportion of paid work, unpaid care and domestic work persisted following the large-scale shift to working from home during periods of pandemic-mandated restrictions in Australia, the UK, the US and other countries (Collins et al., 2020; Craig & Churchill, 2020; Power, 2020). In fact, the closure of schools and childcare facilities and the unavailability of in-home help during times of pandemic restrictions led to an increase in the time spent by women performing unpaid care work (Andrew et al., 2020; Pozzan & Cattaneo, 2020; Seedat & Rondon, 2021).

Unsurprisingly, the increased time spent by women performing unpaid care and domestic work during the pandemic contributed to poorer mental health outcomes for women. An Australian study by Hammarberg et al. (2020) investigated the prevalence of symptoms of depression and anxiety during the first month of pandemic restrictions in 2020. The study found that women were spending more time providing unpaid care work during these periods and had higher rates of clinically significant symptoms of depression and anxiety than men (Hammarberg et al., 2020). These observations suggest that the disproportionate amount of unpaid care work performed by women not only increases the mental health burden of such care but also places them at higher risk of poor mental health.

The DFV workforce in Victoria is highly gendered with 80.5% of the workforce made up of women (Family Safety Victoria, 2017). Aligning with recent research about women bearing the emotional load of the pandemic, the findings from the second Victorian study indicate that the female-dominated Victorian DFV workforce is no exception to the gendered mental health effects of the COVID-19 pandemic. The practitioners in the second Victorian study reported that the general stresses of living and working through a pandemic, particularly increased childcare and home-schooling responsibilities, added another layer to the mental and emotional challenges of their trauma work. As one practitioner explained:

> It's not just the work that we do and the family violence that we hear constantly, it's the fact that we also have our own families, and our own spouses may have lost their jobs, our kids may have mental health issues as well. So, on top of the work that we do we may have also some personal issues. (Specialist DFV practitioner, focus group participant)

This general rise in mental health issues for women performing unpaid care work during periods of pandemic restrictions is likely to be more pronounced for DFV professionals given their key role in responding to the unfolding shadow pandemic of violence against women. Paid care professions, such as those who work in health and aged care services, are overwhelmingly female dominated and DFV workforces are no exception (Family Safety Victoria, 2017; Wood et al., 2017).

Concluding Thoughts

Given their key role in responding to the unfolding shadow pandemic, DFV professionals reported in the data presented in this chapter seemed to be more vulnerable to distress and mental health problems during the COVID-19 crisis. The psychological consequences of exposure to traumatic experiences through their work with clients affected by DFV were compounded by the highly pressurised conditions of the pandemic, particularly the transition to working remotely from home. During periods of lockdowns, many DFV workers brought their trauma work home and offered care and support for people impacted by DFV in the same space they share with family members and others, oftentimes while caring for children during early childhood education and school closures.

The Victorian case study discussed in this chapter demonstrates that DFV professionals pay a significant cost for providing care to trauma survivors remotely from their homes during crises. Similar findings about the negative impact that the pandemic and working from home has had on DFV workforces has been made by researchers in the UK and US (Women's Aid, 2020; Wood et al., 2022). Like their Australian colleagues, US practitioners working at DFV and sexual assault services during the pandemic said that the transition to working remotely from home disrupted their self-care strategies, particularly debriefing with colleagues after difficult cases (Wood et al., 2022). Similarly, staff working in DFV services in the UK during the initial lockdowns from April to June 2020 reported that the shift to working from home isolated them from their work support teams and presented particular challenges for the female-dominated sector whose workers were attempting to balance unpaid and paid care work (Women's Aid, 2020). Both of these studies also echoed the findings of the Australian case study discussed in this chapter about the difficulties of findings a private space to have sensitive and challenging conversations in their homes about clients' traumatic experiences (Women's Aid, 2020; Wood et al., 2022). Taken together this evidence shows that working remotely from homes during periods of lockdowns gave rise to a range of conditions that adversely impacted on DFV workers' social, emotional and psychological wellbeing.

Significantly, there is increasing recognition that the psychological effects of trauma, such as DFV, extend beyond those directly affected and can impact professionals working with trauma survivors (Brend et al., 2020; Cohen & Collens, 2013; Kulkarni et al., 2013). However, to date organisational support for professionals who provide care for people impacted by trauma is largely based around on-site models of working, and sector discussions around DFV worker wellbeing during the COVID-19 pandemic tend to focus on the self-care strategies and practices that individual workers can employ to safeguard their mental health and wellbeing. An exception is the co-designed *Best Practice Guidelines: Supporting the Wellbeing of Family Violence Workers During Times of Emergency and Crisis* (for further information, see Monash Gender and Family Violence Prevention Centre, Domestic Violence Victoria and Domestic Violence Resource Centre Victoria, 2021). This chimes with Cohen-Serrins's (2021) call for greater attention to the role that organisations can play in managing and mitigating the potential harmful effects of trauma work. To ensure the sustainability of DFV workforces, organisational mental health and wellbeing strategies need to be multi-pronged. At the individual level, policies and practices need to support both on-site and remote workers to proactively manage their mental health and wellbeing through crises. At the institutional level, organisations need to develop emergency plans that prioritise the mental health and wellbeing of workers and actively monitor staff wellbeing. Importantly, organisational policies must be future-oriented and seek to build workforce resilience for future crises.

BIBLIOGRAPHY

Andrew, A., Cattan, S., Dias MC., Farquharson, C., Kraftman, L., Krutikova, S., Phimister, A., & Sevilla, A. (2020). *The gendered division of paid and domestic work under lockdown* (IZA discussion paper No. 13500). http://ftp.iza.org/dp13500.pdf

Bagheri Lankarani, K., Hemyari, C., Honarvar, B., et al. (2022). Domestic violence and associated factors during COVID-19 epidemic: An online population-based study in Iran. *BMC Public Health, 22*(1), 774. https://doi.org/10.1186/s12889-022-12536-y

Blake, H., Gupta, A., Javed, M., Wood, B., Knowles, S., Coyne, E., & Cooper, J. (2021). COVID-well study: Qualitative evaluation of supported wellbeing centres and psychological first aid for healthcare workers during the COVID-19 pandemic. *International Journal of Environmental Research and Public Health, 18*(7), 3626. https://doi.org/10.3390/ijerph18073626

Boserup, B., McKenney, M., & Elkbuli, A. (2020). Alarming trends in US domestic violence during the COVID-19 pandemic. *The American Journal of Emergency Medicine, 38*(12), 2753–2755. https://doi.org/10.1016/j.ajem.2020.04.077

Boxall, H., Morgan, A., & Brown, R. (2020). *The prevalence of domestic violence among women during the COVID-19 pandemic* (Statistical Bulletin No. 28). Australian Institute of Criminology. https://www.aic.gov.au/publications/sb/sb28

Brend, D. M., Krane, J., & Saunders, S. (2020). Exposure to trauma in intimate partner violence human service work: A scoping review. *Traumatology, 26*(1), 127–136. https://doi.org/10.1037/trm0000199

Cabarkapa, S., Nadjidai, S. E., Murgier, J., & Ng, C. H. (2020). The psychological impact of COVID-19 and other viral epidemics on frontline healthcare workers and ways to address it: A rapid systematic review. *Brain, Behavior and Immunity—Health, 8*, 100144. https://doi.org/10.1016/j.bbih.2020.100144

Campbell, A. M. (2020). An increasing risk of family violence during the Covid-19 pandemic: Strengthening community collaborations to save lives. *Forensic Science International: Reports, 2*(4), 100089–100030.

Carrington, K., Morley, C., Warren, S., Ryan, V., Ball, M., Clarke, J., & Vitis, L. (2021). The impact of COVID-19 pandemic on Australian domestic and family violence services and their clients. *Australian Journal of Social Issues, 56*, 539–558. https://doi.org/10.1002/ajs4.183

Choi, G. (2011). Secondary traumatic stress of service providers who practice with survivors of family or sexual violence: A national survey of social workers. *Smith College Studies in Social Work, 81*, 101–119. https://doi.org/10.1080/00377317.2011.543044

Cohen, K., & Collens, P. (2013). The impact of trauma work on trauma workers: A metasynthesis on vicarious trauma and vicarious posttraumatic growth. *Psychological Trauma: Theory, Research, Practice and Policy, 5*(6), 570–580.

Cohen-Serrins, J. (2021). How COVID-19 exposed an inadequate approach to burnout: Moving beyond self-care. In C. Tosone (Eds.), *Shared trauma, shared resilience during a pandemic—Essential clinical social work series.* Springer. https://doi.org/10.1007/978-3-030-61442-3_27

Collins, C., Landivar, L., Ruppanner, L., & Scarborough, W. (2020). COVID-19 and the gender gap in work hours. *Gender, Work & Organisation, 28*(S1), 101–112. https://doi.org/10.1111/gwao.12506

Craig, L., & Churchill, B. (2020). Dual-earner parent couples' work and care during COVID-19. *Gender Work and Organisation, 28*, 66–79. https://doi.org/10.1111/gwao.12497

Department of Health. (2020). *2022 aged care workforce census report.* Australian Government. https://www.health.gov.au/sites/default/files/documents/2021/09/2020-aged-care-workforce-census.pdf

Dow, A. (2020, 15 September). Pandemic distress drives some health workers to ponder career change. *The Age.* http://www.theage.com.au/national/pandemic-distress-drives-some-health-workers-to-ponder-career-change-20200914-p55vgo.html?btis

Ervin, J., Taouk, Y., Fleitas Alfonza, L., Hewitt, B., & King, T. (2022). Gender differences in the association between unpaid labour and mental health in employed adults: A systematic review. *The Lancet Public Health, 7*(9), E775–E786. https://doi.org/10.1016/S2468-2667(22)00160-8

Family Safety Victoria. (2017). *Census of workforces that intersect with family violence.* Victorian Government. https://www.vic.gov.au/family-violence-workforce-census

Figley, C. R. (Ed.). (1995). *Compassion fatigue: Coping with secondary traumatic stress disorder in those who treat the traumatized.* Brunner Mazel.

Hammarberg, K., Tran, T., Kirkman, M., & Fisher, J. (2020). Sex and age differences in clinically significant symptoms of depression and anxiety among people in Australia in the first month of COVID-19 restrictions: A national survey, *BMJ, 10*(11), e042696. https://doi.org/10.1136/bmjopen-2020-042696

International Labour Office (ILO). (2018). *Care work and care jobs for the future of decent work.* https://www.ilo.org/wcmsp5/groups/public/---dgr eports/---dcomm/---publ/documents/publication/wcms_633135.pdf

John, N., Casey, S. E., Carino, G., & McGovern, T. (2020). Lessons never learned: Crisis and gender-based violence. *Developing World Bioethics, 20*(2), 65–68. https://doi.org/10.1111/dewb.12261

Joshi, A., Paterson, N., Hinkley, T., & Joss, N. (2021). *The use of telepractice in the family and relationship services sector* (CFCA Paper 57). Australian Institute of Family Studies. https://aifs.gov.au/sites/default/files/public ation-documents/2104_cfca_57_the_use_of_telepractice_in_the_family_and_ relationship_services_sector_0.pdf

Killian, K. D. (2008). Helping till it hurts? A multimethod study of compassion fatigue, burnout, and self-care in clinicians working with trauma survivors. *Traumatology (Tallahassee, Fla.), 14*(2), 32–44. https://doi.org/10.1177/ 1534765608319083

Kinman, G., Teoh, K., & Harriss, A. (2020). Supporting the well-being of healthcare workers during and after COVID-19. *Occupational Medicine, 70*(5), 294–296. https://doi.org/10.1093/occmed/kqaa096

Kulkarni, S., Bell, H., Hartman, J. L., & Herman-Smith, R. L. (2013). Exploring individual and organizational factors contributing to compassion satisfaction, secondary traumatic stress, and burnout in domestic violence service providers. *Journal of the Society for Social Work and Research, 4*(2), 114–130. https://doi.org/10.5243/jsswr.2013.8

Lee, J. J., & Miller, S. E. (2013). A self-care framework for social workers: Building a strong foundation for practice. *Families in Society, 94*(2), 96–103. https://doi.org/10.1606/1044-3894.4289

Lee, J., Flint, J., & McIntosh, J. (2017). *E-screening to connect the dots on risks to family wellbeing: A literature review.* Paper presented at the Family & Relationship Services Australia National Conference. http://frsa.org.au/wp-con tent/uploads/2018/01/FFRSA-conference-ejournal-4.pdf

Martin, J., McBride, T., Masterman, T., Pote, I., Mokhtar, N., Oprea, E., & Sorgenfrei, M. (2020). *Covid-19 and early intervention evidence, challenges and risks relating to virtual and digital delivery.* Early Intervention Foundation. https://www.eif.org.uk/report/covid-19-and-early-int ervention-evidence-challenges-and-risks-relating-to-virtual-and-digital-delivery

McCann, I. L., & Pearlman, L. A. (1990). Vicarious traumatisation: A framework for understanding the psychological effects of working with victims. *Journal of Traumatic Stress, 3*, 131–149. https://doi.org/10.1007/BF00975140

Monash Gender and Family Violence Prevention Centre, Domestic Violence Victoria & Domestic Violence Resource Centre Victoria. (2021). *Best practice guidelines: Supporting the wellbeing of family violence workers during times of emergency and crisis*. Monash University. https://doi.org/10.26180/146050 05.v1

Moreira da Silva, J. (2019, March 18). *Why you should care about unpaid care work*. OECD Development Matters. https://oecd-development-matters.org/2019/03/18/why-you-should-care-about-unpaid-care-work

Morran, D. (2008). Firing up and burning out: The personal and professional impact of working in domestic violence offender programmes. *Probation Journal, 55*(2), 139–152. https://doi.org/10.1177/0264550508090272

Pfitzner, N., Fitz-Gibbon, K., & True, J. (2020a). *Responding to the 'shadow pandemic': Practitioner views on the nature of and responses to violence against women in Victoria, Australia during the COVID-19 restrictions*. Monash University. https://doi.org/10.26180/5ed9d5198497c

Pfitzner, N., Fitz-Gibbon, K., McGowan, J., & True, J. (2020b). *When home becomes the workplace: Family violence, practitioner wellbeing and remote service delivery during COVID-19 restrictions*. Monash University. https://doi.org/10.26180/13108352

Pfitzner, N., Fitz-Gibbon, K., & Meyer, S. (2022a). Responding to women experiencing domestic and family violence during the COVID-19 pandemic: Exploring experiences and impacts of remote service delivery in Australia. *Child & Family Social Work, 27*(1), 30–40. https://doi.org/10.1111/cfs.12870

Pfitzner, N., Fitz-Gibbon, K., & True, J. (2022b). When staying home isn't safe: Australian practitioner experiences of responding to intimate partner violence during COVID-19 restrictions. *Journal of Gender-Based Violence,* 1–18. https://doi.org/10.1332/239868021X16420024310873

Piquero, A. R., Wesley, G. J., Jemison, E., Kaukinen, C., & Knaul, F. M. (2021). Domestic violence during COVID-19: Evidence from a systematic review and meta-analysis. *Journal of Criminal Justice, 74*, 101806. https://doi.org/10.1016/j.jcrimjus.2021.101806

Pozzan, E., & Cattaneo, U. (2020). *Women health workers: Working relentlessly in hospitals and at home*. International Labour Organisation. https://www.ilo.org/global/about-the-ilo/newsroom/news/WCMS_741060/lang—en/index.htm

Power, K. (2020). The COVID-19 pandemic has increased the care burden of women and families. *Sustainability: Science, Practice and Policy, 16*(1), 67–73. https://doi.org/10.1080/15487733.2020.1776561

Preti, E., Di Mattei, V., Perego, G., Ferrari, F., Mazzetti, M., Taranto, P., Di Pierro, R., Madeddu, F., & Calati, R. (2020). The psychological impact of epidemic and pandemic outbreaks on healthcare workers: Rapid review of the evidence. *Current Psychiatry Reports, 22*(43). https://doi.org/10.1007/s11920-020-01166-z

Rmandic, S., Walker, S., Bright, S., & Millsteed, M. (2020). *Police-recorded crime trends in Victoria during the COVID-19 pandemic*. Crime Statistics Agency (Vic). https://apo.org.au/sites/default/files/resource-files/2020-09/apo-nid308473.pdf

Sainato. (2020, 23 September). 'I cry before work': US essential workers burned out amid pandemic. *The Guardian*. https://www.theguardian.com/us-news/2020/sep/23/us-essential-workers-coronavirus-burnout-stress

Sandberg, S., & Thomas, R. (2020, May 7). Sheryl Sandberg: The coronavirus pandemic is creating a 'double double shift' for women. Employers must help. *Fortune*. https://fortune.com/2020/05/07/coronavirus-women-sheryl-sandberg-lean-in-employers-covid-19/

Sanghera, J., Pattani, N., Hashmi, Y., Varley, K., Cheruvu, M., Bradley, A., & Burke, J. (2020). The impact of SARS-CoV-2 on the mental health of healthcare workers in a hospital setting-A Systematic Review. *Journal of Occupational Health, 62*(1), e12175. https://doi.org/10.1002/1348-9585.12175

Seedat, S., & Rondon, M. (2021). Women's wellbeing and the burden of unpaid work. *BMJ, 374*, n1972. https://doi.org/10.1136/bmj.n1972

Storen, R., & Corrigan, N. (2020). COVID-19: *A chronology of state and territory government announcements (up until 30 June 2020)* (Research paper series 2020–2021). Department of Parliamentary Services. https://parlinfo.aph.gov.au/parlInfo/download/library/prspub/7614514/upload_binary/7614514.pdf

Stuijfzand, S., Deforges, C., Sandoz, V., Sajin, C. T., Jaques, C., Elmers, J., & Horsch, A. (2020). Psychological impact of an epidemic/pandemic on the mental health of healthcare professionals: A rapid review. *BMC Public Health, 20*, 1230. https://doi.org/10.1186/s12889-020-09322-z

Tarshis, S., & Baird, S. L. (2019). Addressing the indirect trauma of social work students in Intimate Partner Violence (IPV) field placements: A framework for supervision. *Clinical Social Work Journal, 47*, 90–102. https://doi.org/10.1007/s10615-018-0678-1

Women's Aid. (2020). *A perfect storm: The impact of the covid-19 pandemic on domestic abuse survivors and the services supporting them*. Women's Aid. https://www.womensaid.org.uk/wp-content/uploads/2020/08/A-Perfect-Storm-August-2020-1.pdf

Wood, L., Schrag, R.V., Baumler, E., Hairston, D., Guillot-Wright, S., Torres, E., & Temple, J. R. (2022). On the front lines of the COVID-19 pandemic: Occupational experiences of the intimate partner violence and sexual assault workforce. *Journal of Interpersonal Violence, 37*(11–12), NP9345–NP9366. https://doi.org/10.1177/0886260520983

Wood, L., Wachter, K., Wang, A., Kammer-Kerwick, M., & Busch-Armendariz, N. B. (2017). *The victim services occupation, information, and compensation*

experiences survey (VOICE): Technical Report. https://repositories.lib.ute
xas.edu/bitstream/handle/2152/77464/VOICE-Technical-Report.pdf?seq
uence=2&isAllowed=y

Yaker, R. (2020). *Securing the safety and wellbeing of women frontline healthcare
workers in the COVID-19 response.* https://gbvguidelines.org/en/docume
nts/securing-the-safety-and-wellbeing-of-women-frontline-healthcare-wor
kers-in-the-covid-19-response/

CHAPTER 7

Justice Under Lockdown

Abstract This chapter provides a cross-country exploration of policing and court responses to domestic and family violence during the COVID-19 pandemic. While traditional policing and court response models were disrupted during the pandemic, many police forces and courts adapted their practices, building on already existing digital and remotely enabled options to ensure access to justice was maintained throughout the pandemic. Using empirical data from England and Wales as a case study, this chapter examines the ongoing viability of these options for the delivery of justice, especially for those experiencing DFV, and considers the preparedness of criminal justice systems for future crises.

Keywords Courts · Police · Access to justice · Domestic abuse · Digital justice

INTRODUCTION

Following the World Health Organisation's (WHO) declaration of a global health crisis in March 2020—demanding social distancing and self-isolation—many criminal justice jurisdictions were quick to pivot to alternative modes of delivering justice (Legg & Song, 2021). This shifting

N. Pfitzner et al., *Violence Against Women During Coronavirus*,
https://doi.org/10.1007/978-3-031-29356-6_7

terrain in the delivery of justice comprised a range of responses and innovations some of which were either already in place or were being experimented with. The use of video links for parole hearings, pre-recorded interviews for witnesses deemed vulnerable, other technology-assisted practices enabling remote hearings, and police use of body-worn cameras are just a few examples of the shift towards what might be referred to as 'digital justice'. Nevertheless, the speed at which criminal justice systems pivoted to these forms of delivery during the pandemic was a newer experience for many, with some justice systems better placed to meet these demands than others.

Of course, it is also important to note that by the time the COVID-19 pandemic was taking its toll on formal justice delivery processes, the more informal presence of what Wood et al. (2019) have called 'viral justice' (social media campaigns calling offenders to account), especially in relation to intimate partner violence, was already being felt (see also Fairbairn & Spencer, 2018). However, in this chapter the focus of concern will be on documenting the efficacy and impact of the move toward the online delivery of more formal justice processes in responding to women living with violence(s). Attention, rather, is primarily on policing and criminal court responses during and since the implementation of various forms of public health-driven responses in several different jurisdictions using evidence from England and Wales and Australia as illustrative case studies. To better understand the impact of this shifting terrain on the delivery of more formal justice responses to women, it is important to set these developments within the context of, firstly, a brief overview of the already existing arguments for and against the greater use of the digital in the delivery of justice and, secondly, what was already known about women victim-survivor's expectations of policing and criminal justice processes. Perhaps expressed more abstractly, it is difficult to fully appreciate justice under lockdown without some sense of what Fraser (2009) might call the 'what' and 'who' of justice systems: what is justice for and whose interests are served by it. A brief overview of the arguments for and against digital justice existing prior to the call for justice innovations consequent to the pandemic is first examined.

Digital Justice Before and During the COVID-19 Pandemic

Building on the already existing technological-facilitated practices in the justice system (some of which are listed above), Susskind (2019) makes a compelling case for criminal justice learning lessons from the move towards the digital in civil law. In doing so, Susskind adds some significant weight to the view that remote communities' access to justice is improved by enhanced use of digital responses. Indeed, Genn (2017, p. 3) provides an impressive and convincing list of potential advantages of shifting the work of the courts to an online format including easier document handling and instantaneous information sharing. However, when thinking about the specific issue of access to justice, Genn goes on to observe:

> The key challenge is always to find a balance between rules that will deliver uncomplicated, fair processes and the best chance of a **substantively just** outcome. **The public justice system is founded on different principles from mediation, ODR, EBay, Resolver and other private processes. Parties are not both volunteers. One side may be forced into the process against its will. The public courts are the necessary fall-back when voluntary negotiation over disputes is not possible or has failed.** (NB. Emphasis in the original). (Genn, 2017, p. 7)

Genn (2017) raises some important issues echoing the questions raised earlier by Fraser (2009) concerning the 'what' and 'who' of the criminal justice system. When these questions are placed in the context of women's experiences of criminal justice, especially those living with violence, they become particularly pertinent. Thus, it is important to not assume that access to justice and what that means in terms of who obtains such access and how such justice is delivered to them, is made easier through digital justice options than more conventional justice processes especially for women living with violence. These questions sit in the background in the discussion that follows.

A recent study by Stanford Law School (2021), examining the consequences of the shift to the use of virtual courts in the US during the COVID-19 pandemic, echoed the findings of other studies on the use of video conference/teleconferencing in the justice process. While finding some examples of good practice, this study comments:

> Worryingly, both our study and the literature imply that the use of virtual court proceedings can lead to negative consequences for defendants and for the justice system's legitimacy. Our qualitative interviews and quantitative surveys converge on this point. Defense attorneys responding to the open-ended questions on the survey consistently reported that virtual proceedings dehumanize their clients and lead their clients to distrust the criminal justice system. Proceedings were said to be "devoid of any humanity" or have "a reality TV feel." (Stanford Law School, 2021, p. 170)

In addition, the Stanford report comments on the importance of video quality, questions of investment in technology (also commented on by Genn, 2017), the impact on the nature and influence of non-verbal communication and the resultant impoverishment of client communication. All of which carry implications for claimants, witnesses and defendants and all are features of the *what* and the *who* of the justice process.

A survey of the criminal justice response to the pandemic in several African countries conducted by Muntingh et al. (2022) revealed similar and different issues to those reported in the Stanford (2021) study. They found that confusion arose in those jurisdictions that sought to prioritise urgent cases concerning what counted as urgent:

> Most countries (except for Mozambique) used virtual proceedings to mitigate against the loss of court time. Whilst this is considered a good practice which can be replicated in the future due to its cost-effectiveness and efficiency, limited infrastructure, lack of training and in some cases electricity outages made implementation difficult and often frustrated proceedings. (Muntingh et al., 2022, p. 16)

Issues such as these contributed to subsequent backlogs in the system and over-crowding in pre-trial detention centres. In Canada, Puddister and Small (2020) reported greater resistance in shifting towards the digital during the pandemic. There the justice system expressed a preference for delay rather than so-called 'trial by zoom' except in instances where decisions were deemed urgent—that is, involved rights of habeas corpus or involved vulnerable witnesses. Puddister and Small also point to the greater practical access challenges for remote and rural communities for use of the digital, given their overall poorer access to the internet, for example. Similar pre-pandemic resistance to remote hearings had been reported in England and Wales with the kinds of problems being identified ranging from poor internet connections to poor WiFi, poor equipment and the alienation of a wide range of court users (Institute for Government (IFG), 2020). However, as is discussed later in this chapter, the need to respond during the pandemic arguably overrode some of these concerns (see Rossner et al., 2021). Further, in an experimental study of a virtual court, Rossner and Tait (2021, p. 18) concluded 'that a well-designed distributed court can communicate a sense of equality and shared experience among remote participants in a criminal hearing'.

While many jurisdictions had already started to embrace the use of digital technology in the delivery of the justice process, the extent to which these moves were hastened or resisted during the pandemic was varied and variable. In some respects, the jury is still out on the efficacy of such moves with some problems remaining intransigent to a greater or lesser extent depending upon the nature of the jurisdiction concerned and the resources available for technological investment. In some respects, the principles of a criminal justice system, as alluded to by Genn, have remained somewhat blurred in the drive to keep justice systems working both during and after the pandemic. Meanwhile many jurisdictions, as reported by Muntingh et al. (2022), remain challenged by a backlog of cases built up prior to, during and post pandemic (see inter alia Godfrey et al., 2022a, 2022b). Interestingly in much of this debate about digital justice—except for a wide range of work on police use of body-worn cameras (for a review in relation to DFV, see Pfitzner et al., 2020)—policing responses have largely been absent from this discussion, as have the challenges for this mode of justice delivery for women living with violence. This latter issue is discussed next.

WOMEN AND (DIGITAL) JUSTICE

There is well-established evidence on the tensions which exist for women living with violence in looking to criminal justice as a means of resolving problems in their lives. The mismatch between women's expectations of justice, the delivery of justice and even the different ways in which justice processes contribute to furthering violence in their lives have been differently referred to as 'kaleidoscopic' (McGlynn & Westmarland, 2019), 'white man's justice' (Hudson, 2006) and 'systems abuse' (Douglas, 2018). These terms have been used to describe justice processes in which women always appear as 'unexpected subjects' (Gribaldo, 2021) and/or 'imperfect victims' (Goodmark, 2021). This mismatch between the expectation and experience of criminal justice has perhaps become more complex as the reach of the digital has become ever more pervasive in everyday life.

The pervasiveness of digital technology extends into women's experiences of violence(s) in which things like tracking devices in mobile phones and cars, online stalking and harassment, and the abusive use of image sharing have become constituent elements of how they navigate their lives. In the contemporary world, as Harris (2018) has pointed out, experiences are now not limited by time, place or space. Equally unlimited are some of the evidential requirements made of women when making complaints of abuse. Thus, mobile phone data, for example, can become part of the evidence presented before a court when establishing respective understandings of consent in cases of rape. In some respects, the turn to digital technology in everyday life alongside its increasing presence in criminal justice, arguably, for many women has just meant more of the same: ongoing abuse differently articulated and frequently exacerbated by the criminal justice process. In a telling but differently nuanced way, digital abuse, like other forms of violence is 'just part of life' (Genn, 1988).

At the same time, of course, the increasing presence and influence of social media has in some ways also afforded an opportunity for the expression of different forms as justice. Referred to above, and by Wood et al. (2019), as 'viral justice', the #MeToo campaign stands as testimony to the capacity of social media to act as a forum for alternative responses calling to account in relation to sexual violence (Walklate, 2020), which Cossins (2020) regards as a significant moment in changing the conversation about such violence(s) for men and women. Though these too have the potential for the expression of more punitive responses as well as less punitive ones (Walklate, 2019). Nevertheless, the turn to the digital in all its forms had already begun to change both formal and informal justice practices across a panoply of problematic behaviours, such as DFV, rendering some practitioner responses more ready than others to embrace the potential of the online world. Thus, when faced by the requirements of the pandemic, with many women already cognisant and skilled in the use of digital platforms, the stage was set for a further embrace of digital justice.

In an early assessment of the challenges posed for access to justice, UN Women (2020) offered a holistic overview of these challenges and the place of responding to DFV within them. The following sections of this chapter discuss two themes within these challenges: policing and the courts. By way of illustrating wider international trends in responding to DFV the following discussion draws on empirical work conducted in England and Wales as a case study.[1]

LOCKDOWN TIMELINE IN THE UK: AN OVERVIEW

In England the first national lockdown ran from 23 March 2020, relaxed on 23 June 2020 with variations in Wales, Scotland and Northern Ireland. This lockdown closed all non-essential businesses with people being required to stay at home except for buying food and for medical reasons. Most restrictions across the UK were lifted on 4 July only to be tightened again between July and September with some local areas experiencing higher levels of restrictions referred to as local lockdowns. A second national lockdown was reintroduced on 5 November 2020 in England (with variations elsewhere in the UK) with a tiered system of restrictions operational in December. However, by 30 December 2020, 75% of the country was under the highest tier of restrictions (including limits on how many people could gather in public and private places, attend funerals and so on). A third national lockdown was introduced across the country on 6 January 2021, with restrictions very similar to those of the first (especially the requirement to stay at home). These restrictions started to be lifted on 8 March 2021 but were not fully lifted until July 2021 to allow enough people to receive their first COVID-19 vaccination (for fuller details of the nature and extent of restrictions imposed in the UK, see Brown & Kirk-Wade, 2021).

LOCKDOWN JUSTICE: POLICING RESPONSES TO DFV IN ENGLAND AND WALES

As Halford and Smith (2022) point out there remains ongoing uncertainty as to the extent to which the public health responses to the pandemic resulted in increasing demands on the police both in England and Wales and globally. What is more certain is the impact these responses

---

[1] This work was funded by the Economic and Social Research Council (grant number ES/V00476X/1) and was conducted from June 2020 to December 202 covering the whole of the time period in which lockdown and other restrictions were being managed.

had on support and other services (see Chapter 5). Studies focusing on the impact on policing reveal contradictory trends in different locations (see inter alia Halford & Smith, 2022; Bourgault et al., 2021; and Chapter 1)—some outlined an increase in reported incidents, some a decrease and others no change. A study by Ivandic et al. (2020) added some complexity to this picture by pointing to an increase in third-party reporting and a decrease in ex-partner violence in their study of data from the Metropolitan Police (UK).

Globally such variations are to be expected given differences in cultural relationships with policing. Lack of clarity in relation to such figures reported to and recorded by the police notwithstanding, it is the case that demands on policing in general changed quickly in many jurisdictions during the pandemic. On the one hand under different restrictions on movement in different places the overall pattern of crime changed (less night-time economy crime, street crime and so on) with many police forces being additionally charged with ensuring compliance with lockdown restrictions. On the other hand, maintaining 'business-as-usual' innovative thinking and practice was required to deliver a range of tasks associated with policing. This was especially the case in relation to responding to DFV. In many jurisdictions this was the moment when police forces pivoted to the use of digital technologies in ways that were new to them. It should be noted that little work has offered any in-depth understanding of what these innovative practices looked like and/or how they were experienced by victim-survivors in receipt of them. Nevertheless, acutely aware of the need to remain 'open for business', many police forces in England and Wales pivoted relatively quickly to different ways of responding to DFV. The work conducted by Walklate et al. (2021a, 2021b, 2022) documents some of these practices.

Making sense of innovation in any organisation is neither simple nor straightforward (Weisburd & Braga, 2019). This is particularly tricky in policing, where there is a fundamental reliance upon a 'command and control' model of policy implementation and decision-making. Nonetheless, in the work reported by Walklate et al. (2021b) domestic abuse leads in England and Wales found themselves in a space in which they could exercise both the leverage and the capabilities to create a brokerage role in service delivery reminiscent of social entrepreneurs (Brewer, 2017; Smith, 2020). In England and Wales advertising that they remained open for business for victims of domestic abuse was central. Such practices ranged from using multimedia platforms to reach out to communities to implementing a single point of contact for all domestic abuse support, using Facebook/online forums to reach out to victim-survivors, working with community leaders to access hard-to-reach audiences, and having a police presence in supermarkets, pharmacies and local shops as a way of offering safe spaces for victims to report domestic abuse. Some police forces were also proactive in providing technological aids (like Ring doorbells to high-risk victims),[2] using data analytics to identify high-risk victims with whom contact had been lost, and identifying high-risk offenders and reminding them, where appropriate, of their bail conditions.

One noteworthy move was towards the use of online platforms for multi-agency risk assessment conferences to ensure swift responses to, and the development of, safety plans for high-risk victims. As Walklate et al. (2021a) report, most forces they worked with had made this move, and there was overwhelming enthusiasm for maintaining virtual meetings for this work. The reasons for this ranged from the practical (it is easier to get everyone in the same room at the same time with no travelling issues to negotiate) to perceived improvements in the quality and efficiency of the meetings with improved participation from, and better inter-agency working with, partner organisations. All of this was seen to be to the ultimate advantage of DFV victims. Decisions were made in a more timely, responsive and flexible manner, with all the relevant agencies in the room—a process consistently referred to as 'ideal' especially when it came to Domestic Homicide Reviews (Dawson, 2017).

Offering some insight into a different innovative multi-agency practice, the work reported on by Halford and Smith (2022) examined a pilot project in which Independent Domestic Violence Advisors and Independent Sexual Violence Advocates worked side by side with police officers responding jointly to DFV incidents during the pandemic. This work showed improved victim support and increased engagement with criminal justice on the part of victim-survivors, resulting in improved safety planning and prevention. In a review of support service experiences of working with police forces during this time, Speed et al. (2020, p. 570) also comment: 'Support services report quicker response times and reports of police forces going above and beyond to assist victims with exit strategies where travel is an issue'.

---

[2] Devices that enable people to see who is ringing the doorbell and then can decide whether to open the door.

Many of the practices highlighted above have also been reported on in other European countries (EIGE, 2021), some African countries (Muntingh et al., 2022) and the US (Piquero, 2021). These studies lend weight to the view expressed by the His Majesty's Inspectorate of Constabulary, Fire and Rescue Services (HMICFRS) Report (2021), which states: 'Through innovation, flexibility and adaptability, forces generally successfully maximised the protection of staff while minimising the effect on public service' (HMICFRS Report, 2021, p. 2).

However, if little work has examined how policing practices changed during the pandemic, even less has concerned itself with how such changes were received by victim-survivors. One small-scale study reported by Godfrey et al. (2022a, 2022b) conducted with a southern police force in England and Wales compared victim-survivor views and experiences of face-to-face reporting with online reporting. This study found high victim satisfaction with their contact with police officers in this force, whether interviewed face-to-face or by videoconferencing. In both instances, officers were perceived to be very supportive. For both formats, victim-survivors emphasised the importance of convenience, safety and security for them. They also emphasised the importance of giving victim-survivors a choice over which format was provided to them. While some technical issues prevailed during the roll-out of this practice in this force, these difficulties did not seem to impact upon the victim assessments of their experiences. Nevertheless, the availability of, and investment in, appropriate technological infrastructure was and remains a critical challenge facing court processes during and after the pandemic.

LOCKDOWN JUSTICE: COURT RESPONSES TO DFV IN ENGLAND AND WALES

In England and Wales—somewhat in contrast to policing responses—the courts and other constituent elements of the criminal justice process were rather less than ready to innovate at the start of the pandemic (Speed et al., 2020). As Godfrey et al. (2022a, 2022b) report, crisis management became a key feature of justice delivery for the courts. On 23 March 2020, all jury trials were suspended with His Majesty's Crown Prosecution Service Inspectorate (HMCPSI) (2021) reporting plans to mitigate the impact of lockdowns on the workings of the system. However, by this point newspapers were already reporting that the justice system was in 'meltdown', as the criminal court case backlog passed 37,000 (Dearden, 2020; Syal, 2020). The backlog in the magistrates' courts had, by the end of March 2020, already increased by 32%, from 12,100 to 16,000, and in the Crown Courts by over 40%, from 17,400 to 24,900 during the first few weeks of the first lockdown (HMCPSI, 2021, p. 43). In May 2020, some jury trials were re-initiated in some courts and in June 2020 remote hearings were instituted to deal with all urgent applications including those for bail or to extend custody time limits, and for Domestic Violence Protection Orders (His Majesty's Courts and Tribunal Service [HMCTS], 2020a). Prioritisation of cases became a central plank of response management at this time with cases of domestic abuse listed as second in this list after remand cases. However, by July 2020 it was evident that such crisis management was having little overall impact. Thus, HMCTS (2020b, p. 4) announced a major recovery plan with four pillars: maximising the use of the existing estate (introducing physical screens to ensure safe use of the courts), providing additional capacity through Nightingale Courts, using technology (remote or video hearings) and considering adopting different operating hours (opening the courts on evenings/weekends). The nature of this plan speaks volumes to the readiness and capability of the courts system to respond under the conditions of the pandemic.

Some would say that the recovery plan was 'too little, too late' as by January 2021 magistrates' courts were only just keeping up with new work and reports of cases listed but not to be heard for two to three years were not uncommon (Godfrey et al., 2022a, 2022b). While cases of domestic abuse were second in the list of priorities at this time, the toll on women experiencing DFV and endeavouring to move forward through the criminal justice process with their complaints was considerable. As one police respondent reported on by Godfrey et al. (2022a, 2022b) pointed out in relation to one of their cases:

> DV [domestic violence] assault that occurred in September 2019 and the trial was booked for April 2021. And there was a delay in charging, so the defendant didn't get charged until 2020. But the case management hearing was due to be heard on the 15th of July. And because of COVID-19 restrictions around the court, when my staff updated that in July that had been moved, she was already angry, and she then made the retraction statement and then the case management hearing set the trial and the victim said she's not willing to attend. She's only just managed to get her mental health back on track and she is not going to put her mental health

in jeopardy by waiting for the trial … To tell them that it's going to take
12 to 18 months for it to come to a conclusion—for them I personally
don't think that's probably worth it. (Witness care officer, Southern Force
2)

This above quote appropriately illustrates the challenges for those
willing to participate with the criminal justice process, not only under
pandemic conditions but also more generally. Victim-survivor reluctance
to engage with criminal justice is well documented. Keeping victim-
survivor witnesses on board with the criminal justice process as the
possibility of cases being heard recede into the future is a challenge
(Hester, 2006). As Godfrey et al. (2022a, 2022b, p. 1050) highlight the
attempts to explain the ongoing backlog in the courts system in England
and Wales as simply artefacts of the process:

> Sounds hollow to victims, especially domestic abuse victims, facing long
> delays in getting their cases heard in court. At worst, it legitimates and
> normalises the criminal justice system's lack of response towards innovation
> and speedy justice all of which preceded COVID-19.

The shift to remote courts and online facilitation of document and
information sharing has been a feature of criminal justice responses in a
range of jurisdictions throughout the pandemic. This shift was pointed
to in African countries (Muntingh et al., 2022), the US (Piquero, 2021),
Australia (McIntyre et al., 2020) and several European countries (EIGE,
2021). The usual 'glacial pace' of change (McIntyre et al., 2020) shifted
in momentum in unprecedented ways and outstripped the pre-pandemic-
era resistance to such practices, particularly on the part of the judiciary
and barristers as documented by several commentators (see inter alia
Stanford Law School, 2021). Moreover, these kinds of changes not only
penetrated the criminal justice system but also the family and civil courts
where, in the case of the latter, there was an already ongoing presence of
online resolution processes. In relation to family courts, based on consultations with those working within the family system, Harker and Ryan
(2022) observe:

> The process of "holding up a mirror" to the family justice system in
> this way may be valuable in the long term, not only during a crisis. It
> was particularly striking that the consultations exposed the difficulties that

parents and relatives had with being able to fully participate in court hearings, whether they were parties in public law proceedings or litigants in person. While the nature of remote hearings made participation especially difficult, many of the problems reported by parents and relatives are equally likely to be evident in face-to-face hearings: not feeling "heard," not fully understanding the process etc. (Harker & Ryan, 2022, p. 218)

In other words, the issues of accessibility (in relation to technology, geography and comprehensibility) and participation (being heard and physical presence) added to the questions of personal safety, confidentiality and vulnerability, pertinent to a wide range of victim-witnesses in the justice process but especially in relation to cases involving DFV. These issues have not necessarily been erased in the move towards digital justice. All of this was observed by Byrom (2020). McIntyre et al. (2020) express these concerns in this way:

What steps can be taken to reinstate ordinary judicial principles and processes in the digital sphere ... how do we ensure that adverse practices developed in recent months are not entrenched in a way that persists in the wider movement towards a digital judiciary, long after COVID-19 fades from memory? (McIntyre et al., 2020, p. 201)

The extent to which such 'ordinary justice principles' served women living with violence any better and/or differently in the moves toward digital justice during the pandemic is clearly moot. What is less moot are the questions raised concerning what the legacies of the practices documented above might be.

Lockdown Justice Legacies

It is important to note that in all the policing and criminal justice response examples cited above it is evident that DFV was prioritised in many jurisdictions. While UN Women (2020) are right to observe that much remains to be done—and there is no room for complacency—the high public and media profile given to concerns of a shadow pandemic clearly weighed heavily in the criminal justice responses documented above. The prioritisation given to cases of DFV through the justice process in many jurisdictions stands as testimony to this. However important caveats remain—especially in respect of both what may, or may not, stand the test of time in relation to the innovations discussed above and the effectiveness of the turn to the digital, especially for victim-survivors.

One practice embraced in England and Wales and adopted elsewhere was the move to holding multi-agency risk assessment conferences (MARACs) to the online platform MS Teams. Evidence reported by Walklate et al. (2021a, 2021b) clearly indicated positive support for continuing this practice and for the added value it afforded to victim-survivors: speedier assessments and safety planning with all the appropriate people in the (virtual) room. There was strong policing support to continue this practice. However, as with many other of the innovations discussed above, the focus on being open for business and looking for ways in which to provide support in all the ways that this focus implies, does not erase historically embedded difficulties in some of the practices which pivoted toward the digital. For example, in relation to MARACs police forces took the lead in ensuring these practices continued. Questions remain concerning the extent to which in adopting this leadership role other agencies were encouraged or inhibited from taking part (see also McLaughlin et al., 2018). This observation was made by Bottoms (1990) over three decades ago and has remained a largely unspoken issue since. An associated question also pertinently remains: whose interests lie at the heart of these meetings, the agencies represented in them or the victim-survivor? Moreover, as Welsh (2022) has commented:

> One of the enduring justifications for a partnership response to domestic violence is that women need different services for themselves and their children at different times in the abusive experience but, in the focus on safety planning, the prevailing response is one organised around a very particular time in this experience. It is also organised around a very particular notion of safety – one which is removed from the lived reality of the problem itself. (Welsh, 2022, pp. 16-17)

Arguably, these concerns are not necessarily mutually exclusive but pertain to both modes of managing risk assessment—that is, face-to-face or virtual. Much more work is needed to establish the extent to which these concerns are understood, operationalised and realised before the shift to the digital presumes that the problems of the face-to-face have been erased. McLaughlin et al. (2018) suggest: 'It is time for us to consider whether MARACs still represent the best possible response to multiagency coordination information sharing and planning in relation to domestic violence' (McLaughlin et al., 2018, p. 303). This is particularly pertinent as the volume of work for MARACs has steadily increased and as Welsh (2022) observes has become increasingly focused on those already defined as high-risk to the exclusion of other victim-survivors.

Of course, one of the features central to MARAC practices is good-quality and effective information sharing. The shift to the digital—the use of cloud document sharing practices notwithstanding—makes no presumption that such practices are better quality or more effective.

This is a further lacuna in which more work needs to be done (McCulloch et al., 2020) and is an issue pertaining to both pre- and post-COVID-19 pandemic practices. Moreover, information sharing via the cloud raises further questions of investment in and availability of technological infrastructure, since not all partners to MARACs are adequately endowed. However, effective information sharing, communication and quality data are not just issues for MARACs. They are also issues which have repeatedly emerged in pre-pandemic evaluations of the move toward digital justice in the courts.

For example, in reviewing the evidence on the impact of remote justice with particular reference to vulnerable groups, Byrom (2020) points to major evidence gaps in relation to the impact of partly or fully audio hearings, particularly in relation to family justice, lack of consistency between digital interventions to enable comparisons across different contexts and a complete absence of empirical research on the use of fully video hearings in live cases. If the work of the Stanford Law School (2021) is added to these concerns, then the potential offered by digital responses needs to be examined carefully. Interestingly, as commented above, little of this evaluative work on remote hearings and/or digital justice looks at the development of these practices through the specific lens of victim-survivors of DFV to consider the extent to which such developments match with their expectations of justice. However, as observed at the beginning of this chapter, the mismatch between women's expectations of justice and the delivery of justice is not a new phenomenon.

Concluding Thoughts

The COVID-19 pandemic has revealed much about where both global and local justice responses to DFV are situated within the twenty-first century. While much remains to be done, it is important to take heart from the seriousness with which such violence was addressed during the pandemic. At the same time, however, there are ongoing concerns. Justice backlogs remain in many jurisdictions with the well-known consequences that these have on those living with violence. Lack of investment and appropriate infrastructure remain too. This is not just about technological investment but also the more ordinary, everyday funding needs of support agencies. The suitability of many court estates remains where the provision of separate spaces for defendants and complaints can be crucial. Problems of appropriate information sharing, common understandings of risk and risk assessment, and effective inter-agency cooperation also remain.

Expressed at the beginning of this chapter—by reference to Genn's (2017) observations on access to justice and Fraser's (2009) reminder to reflect on the 'what' and 'who' of justice—it is evident that, despite all the innovation and embrace of the digital exhibited in this chapter, key issues in relation to the bigger question of 'whose justice' for women living with violence remain the same. For example, when responding to DFV whose safety and what understandings of safety are paramount? Who is thought to be vulnerable and why? How is participation in the justice system managed and for whom? When sharing information, what data and whose data is confidential and why? Underpinning all these questions is an implicit recognition that those marginalised by policing and justice systems continue to be so—whether face-to-face or remote (see inter alia Nancarrow, 2019; Goodmark, 2021). The danger lies in the presumption that the digital world erases rather than exacerbates these issues. The jury is still out on this issue.

Bibliography

Bottoms, A. (1990). Crime prevention facing the 1990s. *Policing and Society,* *1*(1), 5–22.

Bourgault, S., Peterman, A., & O'Donnell, M. (2021). Violence against women and children during COVID-19—one year on and 100 papers. In *A fourth research round up centre for global development.* https://www.cgdev.org/sites/default/files/vawc-fourth-roundup.pdf

Brewer, R. (2017). The malleable character of brokerage and crime control: A study of policing, security, and network entrepreneurialism on Melbourne's waterfront. *Policing and Society, 27*(7), 712–731. https://doi.org/10.1080/10439463.2015.1051047

Brown, J., & Kirk-Wade, E. (2021). *Coronavirus: A History of 'lockdown laws' in England* (No. 9068). House of Commons Library. https://researchbriefings. files.parliament.uk/documents/CBP-9068/CBP-9068.pdf

Byrom, N. (2020). What we know about the impact of remote hearings on access to justice: A rapid evidence review. Nuffield Family Justice Observatory. https://www.nuffieldfjo.org.uk/wp-content/uploads/2021/05/nfjo_r emote_hearings_vulnerable-groups_rapid-review_20200506.pdf

Cossins, A. (2020). Feminist Criminology in a Time of 'Digital Feminism': Can the #MeToo Movement Create Fundamental Cultural Change? In S. Walklate, K. Fitz-Gibbon, J. Maher, & J. McCulloch (Eds.), *The Emerald handbook of feminism, criminology and social change* (pp. 69–94). Emerald Publishing. https://doi.org/10.1108/978-1-78769-955-720201007

Dawson, M. (Eds.). (2017). *Domestic homicide and death reviews: An international perspective*. Palgrave-Macmillan.

Dearden, L. (2020, March 29). Coronavirus sends justice system into 'Meltdown' as criminal court case backlog passes 37,000. *The Independent*. https://www.independent.co.uk/news/uk/home-news/coronavirus-justice-system-prisons-court-probation-latest-uk-a9430666.html

Douglas, H. (2018). Legal systems abuse and coercive control. *Criminology & Criminal Justice, 18*(1), 84–99. https://doi.org/10.1177/174889581772 8380

EIGE. (2021). *The Covid-19 pandemic and intimate partner violence against women in the EU*. https://eige.europa.eu/publications/covid-19-pandemic-and-intimate-partner-violence-against-women-eu

Fairbairn, J., & Spencer, D. (2018). Virtualized violence and anonymous juries: Unpacking Steubenville's "Big Red" sexual assault case and the role of social media. *Feminist Criminology, 13*(5), 477–497. https://doi.org/10.1177/ 1557085116687032

Fraser, N. (2009). *Scales of justice*. Polity Press.

Genn, H. (2017, October 6). The Birkenhead lecture: Online courts and the future of justice Gray's Inn. https://www.ucl.ac.uk/laws/sites/laws/files/bir kenhead_lecture_2017_professor_dame_hazel_genn_final_version.pdf

Genn, H. (1988). Multiple victimisation. In M. Maguire & J. Pointing (Eds.), *Victims of crime; A new deal?* (pp. 90–100). Open University Press.

Godfrey, B., Richardson, J., & Walklate, S. (2022a). The crisis in the courts: Before and beyond Covid. *The British Journal of Criminology, 62*(4), 1036–1053. https://doi.org/10.1093/bjc/azab110

Godfrey, B., Richardson, J. William, L & Walklate, S. (2022b). *Evaluation of the use of videoconference interviews for victims of domestic abuse*. https:// www.liverpool.ac.uk/media/livacuk/law-and-social-justice/3research/Rep ort,on,the,Effectiveness,of,Video,Conferences-Sussex,Police-2021.pdf

Goodmark, L. (2021). *Imperfect victims: Criminalized survivors and the promise of abolition feminism*. University of California Press.

Gribaldo, A. (2021). *Unexpected subjects*. HAU Books.

Halford, E., & Smith, J. (2022). Operation provide: A multiagency response to increasing police engagement in cases of intimate partner violence during the COVID-19 pandemic. *Police Practice and Research, 23*(5), 600–613. https://doi.org/10.1080/15614263.2022.2033621

Harker, L., & Ryan, M. (2022). Remote hearings in family courts in England and Wales during Covid-19: Insights and lessons. *Family Court Review, 60*(2), 207–219. https://doi.org/10.1111/fcre.12638

Harris, B. (2018). Spacelessness, spatiality and intimate partner violence: Technology-facilitated abuse, stalking and justice. In J. Maher, S. Walklate, J. McCulloch, & K. Fitz-Gibbon (Eds.), *Intimate partner violence, risk, and security: Securing women's lives in a global world* (pp. 52–70). Routledge.

Hester, M. (2006). Making it through the criminal justice system: Attrition and domestic violence. *Social Policy and Society, 5*(1), 79–80.

HMCPSI. (2021). *Impact of the pandemic on the criminal justice system: A joint view of the criminal justice chief inspectors on the criminal justice system's response to Covid-19*. https://www.justiceinspectorates.gov.uk/hmicfrs/publications/impact-of-the-pandemic-on-the-criminal-justice-system/

HMCTS. (2020a). *HMCTS weekly operational summary on courts and tribunals during coronavirus (COVID-19) outbreak*. https://www.gov.uk/guidance/hmcts-weekly-operational-summary-on-courts-and-tribunals-during-coronavirus-covid-19-outbreak#contents

HMCTS. (2020b). *COVID-19: Update on the HMCTS response for criminal courts in England and Wales*. https://www.gov.uk/government/publications/court-and-tribunal-recovery-update-in-response-to-coronavirus

HMICFRS. (2021). *Policing in the pandemic: The police response to the coronavirus pandemic during 2020*. https://www.justiceinspectorates.gov.uk/hmicfrs

Hudson, B. (2006). Beyond white man's justice: Race, gender and justice in late modernity. *Theoretical Criminology, 10*(1), 29–47. https://doi.org/10.1177/1362480606059981

Institute for Government (IFG). (2020). *Performance tracker 2020: How public services have coped with coronavirus*. https://www.instituteforgovernment.org.uk/sites/default/files/publications/performance-tracker-2020.pdf

Ivandic, R., Kirchmaier, T., & Linton, B. (2020). Changing patterns of domestic abuse during COVID-19 lockdown. *SSRN Electronic Journal*, 1–36. Centre for Economic Performance (Discussion Paper 1729 November). https://cep.lse.ac.uk/pubs/download/dp1729.pdf

Legg, M., & Song, A. (2021). The courts, the remote hearing, and the pandemic. *UNSW Law Journal, 44*(1), 126–165.

McCulloch, J., Maher, J.M. & Pfitzner, N. (2020). Family violence information sharing schemes: Research brief. Monash University. https://doi.org/10.26180/5f6812108d371

McGlynn, C., & Westmarland, N. (2019). Kaleidoscopic justice: Sexual violence and victim-survivors' perceptions of justice. *Social & Legal Studies, 28*(2), 179–201. https://doi.org/10.1177/0964663918761200

McIntyre, J., Olijnyk, A., & Pender, K. (2020). Civil courts and COVID-19: Challenges and opportunities in Australia. *Alternative Law Journal, 45*(3), 195–201. https://doi.org/10.1177/1037969X20956787

McLaughlin, H., Robbins, R., Bellamy, C., Banks, C., & Thackray, D. (2018). Adult social work and high-risk domestic violence cases. *Journal of Social Work, 18*(3), 288–306.

Muntingh, L. J., Mangwanda, J., & Petersen, K. (2022). *Overview and key findings COVID-19 restrictions and the impact on criminal justice and human rights Kenya, Malawi, Mozambique, South Africa & Zambia.* Dullah Omar Institution. https://acjr.org.za/acjr-publications/overview-report-final.pdf

Nancarrow, H. (2019). *Unintended consequences of domestic violence law.* Palgrave-Macmillan.

Pfitzner, N., Fitz-Gibbon, K. & True, J. (2020). *Responding to the 'shadow pandemic': Practitioner views on the nature of and responses to violence against women in Victoria, Australia during the COVID-19 restrictions.* Monash University. https://doi.org/10.26180/5ed9d5198497c

Piquero, A. R. (2021). The policy lessons learned from the criminal justice system response to COVID-19. *Criminology & Public Policy, 20*(3), 385. https://doi.org/10.1111/1745-9133.12562

Puddister, K., & Small, T. A. (2020). Trial by zoom? The response to COVID-19 by Canada's courts. *Canadian Journal of Political Science, 53*(2), 373–377. https://doi.org/10.1017/S0008423920000505

Rossner, M., & Tait, D. (2021). Presence and participation in a virtual court. *Criminology & Criminal Justice.* https://doi.org/10.1177/17488958211017372

Rossner, M., Tait, D., & McCurdy, M. (2021). Justice reimagined: Challenges and opportunities with implementing virtual courts. *Current Issues in Criminal Justice, 33*(1), 94–110.

Smith, R. (2020). The evolution of "entrepreneurial policing": A review of the literature. *Journal of Entrepreneurship and Public Policy, 9*(1), 1–20. https://doi.org/10.1108/JEPP-03-2019-0005

Speed, A., Thomson, C., & Richardson, K. (2020). Stay home, stay safe, save lives? An analysis of the impact of COVID-19 on the ability of victims of gender-based violence to access justice. *The Journal of Criminal Law, 84*(6), 539–572. https://doi.org/10.1177/0022018320948280

Stanford Law School. (2021). *Virtual justice? A national study analyzing transition to remote criminal court*. Stanford Criminal Justice Center. https://law.stanford.edu/wp-content/uploads/2021/08/Virtual-Justice-Final-Aug-2021.pdf

Susskind, R. (2019). *Online courts and the future of justice*. Oxford University Press.

Syal, R. (2020, April 29). Coronavirus could cause "Unprecedented" backlog of court cases. *The Guardian*, https://www.theguardian.com/law/2020/apr/29/coronavirus-could-cause-unprecedented-backlog-court-cases

UN Women. (2020). *COVID-19 and ending violence against women and girls, New York*.https://www.unwomen.org//media/headquarters/attachments/sections/library/publications/2020/issue-brief-covid-19-and-ending-violence-against-women-and-girls-en.pdf?la=en&vs=5006

Walklate, S. (2020). Living in La La Land: "Snowflakes", social change, and alternative responses to sexual assault. In P. Carlen & L. Franca (Eds.), *Justice Alternatives* (pp. 171–184). Routledge.

Walklate, S. (2019). What would a just justice system look like? In W. Dekeseredy & E. Currie (Eds.), *Progressive justice in an age of repression* (pp. 86–98). Routledge.

Walklate, S., Godfrey, B., & Richardson, J. (2021a). Changes and continuities in police responses to domestic abuse in England and Wales during the Covid-19'lockdown.' *Policing and Society, 32*(2), 221–233. https://doi.org/10.1080/10439463.2021.1896514

Walklate, S., Godfrey, B., & Richardson, J. (2021b). Innovating during the pandemic? Policing, domestic abuse and multi-agency risk assessment conferencing (MARACs). *Journal of Adult Protection, 23*(3), 181–190. https://doi.org/10.1108/jap-11-2020-0047

Weisburd, D., & Braga, A. (Eds.). (2019). *Policing innovation*. Cambridge University Press.

Welsh, K. (2022). Long-term partners – Reflections on the shifts in partnership responses to domestic violence. *International Review of Victimology*. https://doi.org/10.1177/02697580211059273

Wood, M., Rose, E., & Thompson, C. (2019). Viral justice? Online justice-seeking, intimate partner violence and affective contagion. *Theoretical Criminology, 23*(3), 375–393.

CHAPTER 8

Conclusion

Abstract This conclusion examines what lessons, if any, can be drawn from adaptations to service delivery and responses during COVID-19 for future policy responses to global and local challenges faced in times of crisis. This chapter draws the book together—paying particular attention to the ways in which the first two years of the COVID-19 pandemic further marginalised certain groups, including women and children who experience domestic and family violence. During this time, the conditions of the global health crisis compounded the already existing impacts of structural inequality. This chapter serves as a 'call to action' for governments worldwide to prioritise women and children's safety and freedom from violence, as governments continue to respond to COVID-19 and other crises. It makes the case that for recovery from a crisis to work, the gendered structural inequalities documented in this book must be front and centre in any policy priorities going forward.

Keywords Covid-19 · Economic insecurity · Gendered impacts · Policy responses · Call to action

© The Author(s) 2023
N. Pfitzner et al., *Violence Against Women During Coronavirus*,
https://doi.org/10.1007/978-3-031-29356-6_8

Introduction

In October 2022, a report published in Australia, entitled Fault Lines, presented the findings of a substantial independent inquiry into Australia's response to COVID-19 (Shergold et al., 2022). The Report identifies four areas where, in the view of the authors, Australia 'should have done better' (Shergold et al., 2022, p. 6) in its response to the pandemic. These four areas covered the provision of fair and equitable economic supports, fewer lockdowns and border closures, keeping schools open and protecting older Australians (Shergold et al., 2022). The 100-page report is among the first of many that will undoubtedly follow in the coming years, designed to scrutinise the pandemic-era actions of countries around the world. Notably, among the 100 pages 'gender' is mentioned once (Shergold et al., 2022, p. 53). One sentence recognises that policies introduced during the pandemic 'could have contributed to approaches that worsened mental health, increased anxiety and triggered family violence' (Shergold et al., 2022, p. 53). This is supported by a single paragraph later in the report which acknowledges that, for some, the COVID-19 pandemic represents a story of 'more domestic violence' and the many structural factors that further increased this risk. Here, the report states:

> For others, COVID-19 will be a story of trauma, isolation and terrifying uncertainty. It will be a story of being locked in overcrowded housing, job loss and missing out on government supports. It will be a story of more domestic violence, increased alcohol abuse, and deteriorating mental and physical health. (Shergold et al., 2022, p. 79)

In contrast, throughout the pages of this book many aspects of the 'domestic violence story' of the COVID-19 pandemic have been told through the presentation of a series of case studies as well as the extensive body of research that is now available. The authors of this book have focused on specific contexts and locations but within this, global questions have also been raised. Unlike the report referenced above—as well as the many policy briefings, public announcements and speeches which predated it—the analysis presented here has centred on gender and vulnerability, bringing to the fore the gendered impacts of political and policy decision-making during the first two years of the COVID-19 pandemic.

Through an exploration of different political and policy responses to COVID-19, and the varied and ongoing impacts of the pandemic, this book has sought to highlight the impacts the COVID-19 pandemic had—and continues to have—on violence against women and children, and the lessons that might be learnt for policy makers moving forward. The book has not sought to present a country-specific analysis (though the significant tilt towards Australian and UK case studies throughout is acknowledged by the authors), but rather to demonstrate that women and children's safety and their experiences of violence during the pandemic have been shared in similar ways across the globe. While many around the world quickly came to adopt the nomenclature 'shadow pandemic', as first characterised by the UN (UN Women, 2020), in the initial stages of the COVID-19 pandemic, responses which considered and centred the safety of women experiencing DFV were seemingly few and far between. This final chapter examines what lessons, if any, can be taken from adaptations to service delivery and other responses that were made during the pandemic, for future crisis management and policy responses.

The Unfolding Pandemic

Much of the analysis offered in this book draws on material which focuses on the nature and extent of the COVID-19 pandemic in early 2020 running through to the end of 2022. The end of 2022 was the point at which many countries moved into the next phase of the pandemic. In this phase, public health policies largely abandoned the frequent use of stay-at-home orders and social movement restrictions shifted towards strategies focused on vaccination and economic recovery. With this in mind, this book is careful to not imply that the pandemic is over. Rather, it is important to note that while case numbers continue to ebb and flow internationally, the consequences of the COVID-19 pandemic are still unfolding. In many ways, these consequences are yet to be fully realised—particularly economically—and the concomitant impact of these consequences will continue to be felt in relation to women's safety.

In order to make sense of the complex ways in which the COVID-19 pandemic can impact on a wide range of aspects of women's lives, it is useful to return to Peterman et al.'s (2020) nine pathways, which highlight the different ways in which the pandemic may have a direct or indirect impact on violence against women and girls. These pathways were outlined in the introduction to this book, though they are worth repeating:

1. economic insecurity and poverty-related stress,
2. quarantines and social isolation,
3. disaster and conflict-related unrest and instability,
4. exposure to exploitative relationships due to changing demographics,
5. reduced health service availability and access to first responders,
6. inability of women to temporarily escape abusive partners,
7. virus-specific sources of violence,
8. exposure to violence and coercion in response efforts, and
9. violence perpetrated against health care workers. (Peterman et al., 2020, p. 5)

While it has not been the intention of this book to interrogate each and every one of these pathways, the material contained throughout demonstrates many of the direct and indirect impacts that Peterman et al. (2020) drew attention to. For example, UN Women (2021) offer a wide-ranging statistical review of the economic and poverty-related stresses experienced during the COVID-19 pandemic. Additionally, Abraham et al. (2022) report that in India:

> Conditional on being in the workforce prior to the pandemic, women were seven times more likely to lose work during the nationwide lockdown, and conditional on losing work, eleven times more likely to not return to work subsequently, compared to men. (Abraham et al., 2022, p. 101)

These are just two among a wealth of studies documenting the consequences beyond ill health of COVID-19, and the impact of policy responses to it on women. Moreover, this analysis demonstrates that impacts such as these are intimately connected with the nature and extent of the violence(s) experienced by women in times of crisis more generally (see Chapter 2). Thus, the gendered nature of the impact of COVID-19 and related public health measures cannot be overlooked. In particular, this analysis draws attention to the existence and impacts of pathways one, two, three, five and six (see Chapters 2, 3, 5 and 6).

The authors of this book are also mindful that, since the onset of the pandemic, many other natural disasters have impacted nations across the globe. This brings to mind the importance of considering our analysis of how women and children's safety is impacted by the COVID-19 pandemic, and the policy responses within the broader context of disasters that are increasingly a feature of a world impacted by climate change.

Peterman et al.'s (2020) framework, while originally written with the pandemic in mind, provides an important way of thinking about the wide range of ways in which disasters of all kinds can have gendered consequences. To this end—as much of the material presented in this book points to—these consequences serve as a warning that when the gendered impacts of public policy during disaster are not given due consideration, the impacts on women's economic security and personal safety are significant with further ongoing consequences for societal and economic recovery. Whether through policy decisions relating to stay-at-home orders, work-from-home recommendations, school closures, changes to the migration system or access to protection via the justice system, the failure—in many countries—to adequately consider women's economic security and personal safety at each point of the COVID-19 pandemic must serve as an example for political leaders who encounter times of disaster in years to come. Importantly, however, this is not solely an issue for attention during disasters. As Parry and Gordon (2021) comment of South Africa:

> It is of the utmost importance that we address IPV, not only as the shadow pandemic of increasing violence against women during COVID-19, but as the overwhelming and devastating pandemic it is for the women in South African society, day after day, hour after hour. (Parry & Gordon, 2021, p. 804)

The high prevalence rate of domestic violence globally (WHO, 2021) highlights the importance for all countries of this statement. Much of what became more visible during the early phase of the COVID-19 pandemic had already been widely documented during other times of crisis and disasters, as discussed in Chapter 2. The intriguing elephant-in-the-room question is: why, if all this was known, was it not taken account of in policy responses?

Nevertheless, regardless of what was already known or what this implies for disasters to come, Peterman et al.'s (2020) first pathway of economic insecurity and poverty-related stress has well and truly taken hold globally as the cost-of-living crisis and the resultant impacts on family stresses have emerged centre stage three years into the pandemic. Again, a failure to acknowledge the gendered impact of this economic crisis represents a political unwillingness to take women's economic and personal safety seriously. As stated by Nazeer and Sharp-Jeffs (2022):

> We're all worried about the cost of living crisis. From interest rates to groceries, utility bills to petrol, everything is getting more expensive. But for some women, this crisis could mean the difference between life and death. Lack of economic safety forces women to stay with abusers longer than they want to, meaning they experience more harm as a result. For those that leave, economic abuse can long continue, preventing women from rebuilding their lives, sometimes for decades. (Nazeer & Sharp-Jeffs, 2022, p. 1)

A survey undertaken in England and Wales by Women's Aid found that 66% of victim-survivors reported that their abuser was using the increase in the cost-of-living as a tool for coercive control, while 50% of victim-survivors noted that the increase in the cost of living was a barrier to leaving their abuser by fear of not being able to financially support children (Nazeer & Sharp-Jeffs, 2022). As revealed in Chapter 2, it is not uncommon for perpetrators to utilise wider circumstances to evolve their tactics of coercion and control. This analysis, undertaken in England and Wales, shows why governments must not interpret the move away from stay-at-home restrictions as meaning that women and children experiencing family violence now enjoy a freedom to leave abusive homes. The act of leaving is, of course, a well-known trigger for violence escalation and intimate partner homicide (see inter alia Dekeseredy et al., 2017). The increasingly trying nature of the economic circumstances within which lives are being lived operates as a new barrier (for some) to help-seeking, and one which policy makers globally must seek to address. That such economic circumstances predictably take their toll on those economically deprived across all societies—and their links with stress, violence and poorer life expectancy—should place women and children at the centre of such concerns (see also the edited collection by Fassin & Fourcade, 2021, discussed in Chapter 1). At this juncture, the elephant in the room becomes a mammoth.

Absent Present Policy

The gendered impacts of the COVID-19 pandemic can be spoken about as universally present. However, while recognising that in many cases the pandemic compounded structural inequities, the analysis presented in this book reveals a tale of two stories, where public health and other policy responses are subjected to closer scrutiny. On the one hand, there were reactive responses, particularly in the early days of the pandemic, where there was little to no consideration given to the safety needs and impacts of women and children experiencing violence. Such reactions saw mass closures of schools and the overnight introduction of stay-at-home restrictions, including curfews, variously enacted in different geographical locations for different periods of time. These responses were sold on the promise of responding to health advice and in the absence of any *guidebook* for managing a global pandemic. Much of this policy making necessitated a trial-and-error approach. In some countries, this reactive policy approach was very quickly challenged by those voices aware of the consequence that stay-at-home/shelter-in-place directives might have on the nature and extent of violence(s) in women's and children's lives. In response to such voices, some jurisdictions quickly provided extra funding support for service providers (see Chapter 2). However, there is a second strand to this story, which speaks to the ongoing absences in policy responses to violence against women. Importantly, these two stories are not separate or separable. They are intertwined. In any one jurisdiction they can exist side-by-side, making the absent present in such policy responses ever more telling.

To be specific—and by way of illustration—it is of value to return to one of the themes addressed in this book: the turn to digital justice and other service responses using the digital world as a means for service delivery. Such policy response options existed in their embryonic form in a wide range of jurisdictions prior to the COVID-19 pandemic (see, in particular, Chapter 7, and the concomitant implications in the use of these mechanisms in working from home for support workers as documented in Chapter 6). This turn to the digital assumes a jurisdictional infrastructure both intra-organisational, across organisational and societal (rural and urban), in which participants are equipped with the skills and resources to enable their participation. The assumptions made here about where, when and who has access to services and support delivered in this way are profound. The absence of clear thinking around the consequences of this policy turn for those marginalised (economically, physically, linguistically, due to homelessness and so on) speaks volumes about who and what the target of such policies are. Elsewhere, Jones (2022) has developed the concept of bureaucratic violence as one way of making sense of the gap between policy promise and its delivery in violence against women in Indonesia. The absent presence of such violence runs deep from the failure to provide appropriately funded alternative housing policies for women wishing to leave abusive relationships to the capacity of different organisations to occupy different planets (Hester, 2011) in their responses to women and children (on the experiences of Indigenous women, also see Stubbs & Wangmann, 2015).

Regardless of the policy emphasis adopted, the pandemic has exposed the historic failure to meaningfully invest in the kind of system infrastructure needed to ensure women's safety. In many jurisdictions, specialist services were required to step in and fill the gap where governments had not built whole-of-system responses to violence against women. For example, as referred to above, the lack of accessible housing options in many countries (see also EIGE, 2021) was apparent in early 2020 even as governments around the world moved to impose 'stay home, stay safe' policies. This failed to consider that for a significant portion of every community, home is not a safe place (see inter alia Summers, 2022). Further, the long-term lack of investment in child-centred services for children and young people experiencing family violence was also apparent as children around the world headed home for long periods of time during COVID-19-related school closures, alongside the absence of a service system skilled to address their safety and support needs.

The reliance on the women's safety sector, made up of women supporting women, is not new in the context of disaster. This is a persistent reality of an infrastructure that, in many places globally, is at best piecemeal and largely reactively focused on victims rather than overarching efforts to identify the deep connections between gender inequality that is sustained by many aspects of social and economic policy. Rather than interrogating what sustains violence, policy responses instead emerge to deal with its aftermath alongside some additional piecemeal funding. This calls to mind the question of how to push beyond and becomes more of a question of how to call nations to account for the conditions that sustain gendered violence.

As detailed throughout this book, this absent policy response has resulted in a lack of a service infrastructure/workforce not prepared for a pandemic—meaning significant pressures were placed upon those specialist practitioners working within systems that were largely disconnected and already overstretched, and heavily reliant on women and primary carers. As the analyses in Chapters 5 and 6 reveal, the women's safety sector undertook significant transformations during the pandemic to ensure the continued delivering of support to women experiencing domestic violence, even where face-to-face provisions, safety planning and risk assessment were not possible. Thus, this pivot has come at a cost—one that is yet to be fully realised.

Concluding Thoughts: The Ongoing Impacts of Global Uncertainty

Building on the earlier discussion of the cost-of-living crisis, this book acknowledges that at the time of writing (2022) the public's attention on the COVID-19 pandemic has in many ways been overshadowed by other global issues. It is a time of significant global uncertainty and change. To this end, while the COVID-19 pandemic represented a 'moment in time focus' throughout 2020 and 2021, the laser-eyed attention of the world has shifted to the war in Ukraine, the fight for women's rights in Iran, the political turmoil in the UK, the winding back of women's reproductive rights in the US—the list goes on. Nevertheless, it is essential to recognise that the ongoing impacts of the pandemic are continuing to have a ripple effect on women's safety and can compound the capacity of individuals and communities to recover.

In this shift to recovery from the pandemic, Carlien Scheele, Director of the EIGE, in a press release issued on International Women's Day, 2021, had this to say:

> Europe will bounce back, as long as gender equality is front and centre of recovery measures. In a small win for gender equality, Member States will have to show how their economic recovery plans promote gender equality in order to access the EU's recovery fund. EIGE can help with that by providing gender statistics, which are crucial to understand the different effects of the pandemic on women and men and assess where the money is most needed. (Scheele, 2021)

This statement reveals a clue into how to manage and move on from this time of global uncertainty: data. One call to action implied in the pages of this book is the availability of data, appropriately disaggregated and collated in order to document the wider impacts of contemporary precarity. Without data, making progress in relation to gender—and all other inequalities—will forever be absent in policy. However, data on its own does not generate change. Having an appropriately co-ordinated and integrated policy framework might. Much has been made, especially in Europe, of the importance of the Istanbul Convention (2011) and its four pillars of action in relation to violence against women and children: prevention, protection, prosecution and integration. This convention is sometimes referred to as a 'gold standard' for action. Such claims notwithstanding, 10 years on this convention has been denounced by Turkey and not yet fully ratified by the EU—a timely reminder that making change is an ongoing enterprise. Speaking at the European Gender Equality Forum on 24 October 2022, the UN Special Rapporteur, Reem Alsalem, called for action plans, resources, implementation plans and coordination in order to move forward on combatting violence(s) against women and children. Much of this is, of course, not new. However, it may be that the light at the end of the pandemic tunnel might, as one critic has pointed out, result in a recognition for 'creativity on many fronts, not least by creating a synergy between feminist theory, evidence gathering, and practice. Together these could add up to much more than the sum of their individual trajectories' (Agarwal, 2021 p. 252). It could even, perhaps, lead to a wider acknowledgement of what Mooi-Reci and Risman (2021) call 'cultural logics'. As they point out in introducing a special issue of the journal *Gender and Society*:

> Most women in opposite-sex couples in most of the world took on more of the extra domestic work and child care during the pandemic. No law required them to do so. No social policy incentivized such behavior. Such is the power of cultural logics that presume women are responsible for caretaking work. But the cross-cultural differences in these studies also suggest that material conditions, government policies such as school opening, and financial support for workers decreased women's burdens. (Mooi-Reci & Risman, 2021, p. 166)

Policies can, and do, make a difference. There is more work to be done.

BIBLIOGRAPHY

Abraham, R., Basole, A., & Kesar, S. (2022). Down and out? The gendered impact of the Covid-19 pandemic on India's labour market. *Economia Politica, 39*, 101–128. https://doi.org/10.1007/s40888-021-00234-8

Agarwal, B. (2021). Reflections on the less visible and less measured: Gender and COVID-19 in India. *Gender & Society, 35*(2), 244–255. https://doi.org/10.1177/08912432211001299

Dekeseredy, W., Draguewicz, M., & Schwartz, M. (2017). *Abusive Endings: Separation and divorce violence against women.* University of California Press.

Europen Institute of Gender Equality (EIGE). (2021). The Covid 19 Pandemic and Intimate Partner Violence Against Women in the EU. www.eige.eur opa.eu

Fassin, D., & Fourcade, M. (Eds.). (2021). *Pandemic exposures: Economy and society in times of coronavirus.* HAU Books.

Hester, M. (2011). The three planet model: Towards an understanding of contradictions in approaches to women and children's safety in contexts of domestic violence. *The British Journal of Social Work, 41*(5), 837–853. http://www.jstor.org/stable/43771471

Jones, B. (2022). Reaching out from the ocean: women's experiences navigating the anti-domestic violence law in Aceh, Indonesia. Doctoral Thesis, University of Melbourne.

Mooi-Reci, I., & Risman, B. J. (2021). The gendered impacts of COVID-19: Lessons and reflections. *Gender & Society, 35*(2), 161–167. https://doi.org/10.1177/08912432211001305

Nazeer, F., & Sharp-Jeffs, N. (2022) With the cost of living crisis preventing women from fleeing abuse, the government must act now to support survivors. 5 October. Women's Aid. https://www.womensaid.org.uk/with-the-cost-of-living-crisis-preventing-women-from-fleeing-abuse-the-govern ment-must-act-now-to-support-survivors/?utm_source=rss&utm_medium= rss&utm_campaign=with-the-cost-of-living-crisis-preventing-women-from-fle eing-abuse-the-government-must-act-now-to-support-survivors

Parry, B. R., & Gordon, E. (2021). The shadow pandemic: Inequitable gendered impacts of COVID-19 in South Africa. *Gender Work Organisations., 28*, 795–806. https://doi.org/10.1111/gwao.12565

Peterman, A., Potts, A., O'Donnell, M., Thompson, K., Shah, N., Oertelt-Prigione, S., & van Gelder, N. (2020). *Pandemics and violence against women and children* (CGD Working Paper 528). Center for Global Development. https://www.cgdev.org/publication/pandemics-and-violence-against-women-and-children

Scheele, C. (2021). COVID-19 derails gender equality gains. Europen Institute of Gender Equality, 5 March. https://eige.europa.eu/news/covid-19-derails-gender-equality-gains

Shergold, P., Broadbent, J., Marshall, I., & Varghese, P. (2022) Fault lines: An independent review into Australia's response to COVID-19. 20 October, Paul Ramsay Foundation. https://www.paulramsayfoundation.org.au/news-resour ces/fault-lines-an-independent-review-into-australias-response-to-covid-19

Stubbs, J., & Wangmann, J. (2015). Competing conceptions of victims of domestic violence within legal processes. In D. Wilson & S. Ross (Eds.), *Crime, victims and policy* (pp. 107–132). Palgrave-MacMillan.

Summers, A. (2022). The choice: Violence or poverty. University of Technology Sydney. https://doi.org/10.26195/3s1r-4977

UN Women. (2020). *The shadow pandemic: Violence against women and girls and COVID-19*. https://www.unwomen.org/en/digital-library/multim edia/2020/4/infographic-covid19-violence-against-women-and-girls

UN Women. (2021). Measuring the shadow pandemic: Violence against women during Covid-19. https://data.unwomen.org/publications/vaw-rga

World Health Organization (WHO). (2021). *Violence against women. Key facts.* 9 March 2021.

INDEX

Zeitfracht Medien GmbH
Ferdinand-Jühlke-Straße 7
99095 Erfurt, Deutschland
produktsicherheit@kolibri360.de